THE
RIGHT
CALL

ALSO BY SALLY JENKINS

The Real All Americans

The State of Jones (coauthored with John Stauffer)

THE
RIGHT
CALL

WHAT SPORTS TEACH US
ABOUT WORK AND LIFE

SALLY JENKINS

GALLERY BOOKS

NEW YORK   LONDON   TORONTO   SYDNEY   NEW DELHI

G

Gallery Books
An Imprint of Simon & Schuster, Inc.
1230 Avenue of the Americas
New York, NY 10020

First Gallery Books hardcover edition June 2023

GALLERY BOOKS and colophon are registered
trademarks of Simon & Schuster, Inc.

For information about special discounts for bulk purchases, please contact Simon & Schuster Special Sales at 1-866-506-1949 or business@simonandschuster.com.

The Simon & Schuster Speakers Bureau can bring authors to your live event. For more information or to book an event, contact the Simon & Schuster Speakers Bureau at 1-866-248-3049 or visit our website at www.simonspeakers.com.

Manufactured in the United States of America

10 9 8 7 6 5 4

Library of Congress Cataloging-in-Publication Data

Names: Jenkins, Sally, author.
Title: The right call : what the athletic mindset teaches us about the art
    of decision making / Sally Jenkins.
Description: First Gallery Books hardcover edition | New York, N.Y. :
    Gallery Books, 2023. | Includes index.
Identifiers: LCCN 2022028417 (print) | LCCN 2022028418 (ebook) |
ISBN 9781982122553 (hardcover) | ISBN 9781982122577 (ebook)
Subjects: LCSH: Sports—Psychological aspects. | Athletes—Training of. |
Athletes—Psychology. | Athletic ability.
Classification: LCC GV706.4 .J45 2023 (print) | LCC GV706.4 (ebook) |
DDC 796.01/9—dc23/eng/20220720
LC record available at https://lccn.loc.gov/2022028417
LC ebook record available at https://lccn.loc.gov/2022028418

ISBN 978-1-9821-2255-3
ISBN 978-1-9821-2257-7 (ebook)

For Mary Carillo,
champion and champion friend,
who's lived all this

Contents

Prologue

Getting Serious about Greatness

The sportswriter's seat is the best in the house. Not because it comes with free popcorn, though it often does, or because it has a better angle on the big game than the average ticket buyer can procure, which it doesn't always. What makes the seat worth coveting is its unpurchasable proximity to greatness in practice. I've not been fool enough to waste that. I take notes.

To witness the clutch shot, the winning throw, or the final strike is just a fractional part of the job. Most of your time is spent at practice, watching the alchemical processes by which coaches and athletes find the right action in the moment. Before and after practice, in the back halls and tunnels of clubhouses, a sportswriter can interview some of the greats and gather insights into the vital matter of their performance under pressure. My friend the TV commentator Lesley Visser has joked that we should title a book *Presumed Intimacy*, because the quest to understand what they do can lead to some pretty intrusive questions. Once, I sat with the NBA's celebrated shooter Stephen Curry after a practice with the Golden State Warriors and, unable to resist, actually heard myself say, "Can I feel your hands?"

Curry obligingly held out his palms. I placed mine on top. Shocked, I felt slabs of rough, coarse, flaking callouses. Somehow, I had expected his hands to be soft. Curry's frame is so sylphlike and flitting, his shot so effortless seeming. But these were the hands of a logger. In that moment, I understood that Curry's ease with a basketball wasn't easy at all. It was produced by two thousand practice shots a week, a labor that rubbed his hands raw.

Encounters like that one brought a fundamental realization: even the most supple-seeming actors are the products of their own agency. Their skills are not a matter of natural talent but attainment. Most important, their alertness and executive cool in critical moments is earned and learned.

Which suggests that others can learn it, too, even those of us who test our limits at a desk. This provocative connection was reinforced by a conversation with Tennis Hall of Famer Rod Laver one day sitting on a bench in the outer courts at Wimbledon while reporting a story about Pete Sampras. I asked Laver if all major champions have something in common. Yes, Laver replied. "They're all able to summon their best at the moments when they most need to."[1]

Who wouldn't like to be able to do that, no matter what the profession?

The proximity to champions and champion organizations has unquestionably influenced how I go about my own job. Several years ago, I was assigned by *Sports Illustrated* magazine to do a piece about Billie Jean King's metamorphosis from a great player to a coach, who helped shore up a nerve-prone Martina Navratilova late in her career. After spending time with King, listening to her talk about how tennis was less about talent than about "mastering a craft," I sat down to write.[2] It was one of my first big assignments for the magazine, and as I stared at the blank computer screen I suddenly realized I was gagging. I thought, *Well, that's just great; here you are writing a piece about one of the greatest pressure performers ever and you're choking your guts out.*

I somehow got a publishable piece done. But afterwards it occurred to me that deadline writing was a form of performance under pressure, too. And I began to think about how to do it better, instead of trusting to flair, or a jolt of inspiration. I found myself thinking, *If you're ambitious about something, why wouldn't you behave half as committedly about your ability as any athlete does?*

That simple shift in perspective caused me to go back over years of experiences with coaches and athletes and reframe them, revise my opinion of what matters about them. Too often we're overawed by them for the wrong things. We celebrate their glamour and ascribe all kinds of idealized qualities to them they don't really possess, while ignoring those they do, such as perseverance. The laziest-seeming pro athlete works much harder than the average person, day in and day out, to get better, and is more forthright when it comes to confronting their unevenness under pressure. Too often, we overlook the real merits of the athletic mindset and tell ourselves that it interferes with more serious matters. We don't do that with any other disciplines in the humanities, arts or sciences, or business. What a discriminatory cheat.

When I was a child, I had the usual cases of hero worship. I was exposed to some idols early, thanks to my father, the Hall of

Fame sportswriter Dan Jenkins, who towed me to various events as he wrote prizewinning pieces for *Sports Illustrated* and then *Golf Digest*. Along the way he tried to strip away the false sentiment and children's literature–mythologizing surrounding sports for his readers. As I carried coffee to him in the pressrooms, he would occasionally drop a remark meant to cure me of the same. I took in the lessons only vaguely and half stored them away. Once, he told me that it was "a kind of sin" to waste potential and the real champions never committed it.

On another occasion he said, "A lot of people are afraid to win."

For years, I didn't quite know what he meant by that remark. But one day I mentioned the line to my late friend Pat Summitt, the winner of eight women's basketball championships at the University of Tennessee. "He's right," Pat said. What my father was getting at, Pat explained, was that "some people don't want to keep score, because they'll have to say, 'That's the best I can do.'"[3]

All of the people in these pages have a willingness to say, "That's the best I can do."

Much of the material here has been amassed on assignments for the *Washington Post*, an extremely privileged position that has afforded me more than thirty years of opportunities to go to big events and talk to the people competing in them. Other invaluable experiences also came at *Sports Illustrated*, and ESPN. In a way, this book is a letter of appreciation to the array of strivers I've encountered, whose determination to keep score—even if it means running head-on into their limits—informs my own work.

You spend your whole life writing about coaches and athletes, trying to get impressions of them on to a page, literally stamping them down in letters. But at a certain point somewhere along the line, you realize that *they* have begun to write *you*, and might even shape you into something better, if you let them. Impressions come floating back, bits and pieces of conversations and outtakes from notebooks over the years that gradually began to fit together in something like a meaningful picture. Such as:

Sitting with Charles Barkley, back when he was a young All-Star NBA player for the Philadelphia 76ers, and hearing him say from the bottom of his tremendous heart, "I realize I'm never going to be perfect, but as long as you strive to, at least you're going to get better. I don't ever want to make a mistake and say, 'That's all right.' Because then it becomes a part of you. I don't want mistakes to become a part of my life."[4]

When I first encountered Michael Phelps at the Athens Olympics, I wrote this about him: "If you wander through the fish stalls of Piraeus, you will see dangling rows of calamaris. They all look like Michael Phelps's torso. They have the same tensile, wavy arms, and pulpy slabs of muscle, and apparently, they have the same pulse rate." But what made Phelps truly great, I learned in conversation with him, was his embrace of absolutely drudgery. Phelps's easy rhythm in the water was as much a matter of mental conditioning as physical, the result of years of metronomic laps like musical scales. Practice laps were tedious, but they induced a psychological blankness that Phelps, who struggled with ADHD and anxiety, found relieving. In the water there were no other problems, no complications, no other responsibilities, than to focus on stroke technique and burn rate. That is what allowed him to regulate his pulse and control the messaging system between his body and his brain.

"Let's talk about neuroscience," I said to Phelps, one day.

"Uh-oh," he said, laughing.

"Are you thinking during a race?" I asked.

"No."

"Do you count?"

"Count what?"

Strokes. Laps.

"I mean, I can tell you exactly how fast I'm going because of feel."

That ingrained rhythm gave him a nerveless confidence in races, he said. "When I'm racing," Phelps continued, "I just get in the water and do whatever I've done in workouts."[5]

A young woman in her twenties could have worse assignments than to hang around the towering figures who populated the Women's Tennis Association from the early 1980s on. From Chris Evert and Martina Navratilova to Steffi Graf to Venus and Serena Williams, the tour was a gallery of stunning champions who worked at their crafts with unembarrassed intensity. They were perfectionists on the court, but if you caught them with the right question off of it, they were also bemusingly self-aware, and would delight you by hurling themselves off of pedestals with revealing truthfulness. Asked once by my friend and colleague Mike Lupica if she thought she was pretty, Evert replied, "Just missed." Evert was never the most prepossessing player on the court physically, but you learned from her measured grace that technical mastery was supreme to raw strength every time. "I controlled the point," Evert said to me. "I won my way. I had the opponent on the run. I was the one moving them around."[6]

Those players grew me up as much as any parent ever did. I emerged from their influence with a growing, if not yet not fully articulated, sense that what athletes and coaches have to teach isn't triumphalism. What they teach is that identity is a self-construct. "People who bet on themselves tend to win,"[7] Billie Jean said on one occasion, and you could tell from her tone that she was trying to tell you what mattered most was not the winning but the guts.

I can't stress enough that champions are essentially the product of their own work. Even the most secluded superstars would like to be better understood in this respect. I've never known a winner, not one, who wasn't irritated by the lame idea that they were God-kissed with fortunate gifts. All of them sweat in far greater proportion to anything natural-born in them. Kansas City Chiefs quarterback Patrick Mahomes has an implausibly tensile arm, but the main factors that allowed him to win a Super Bowl by the age of twenty-five were his diligent study and refusal to cheat the grind. When he signed a contract worth half a billion dollars, his idea of how to splurge was to build a fifty-yard field in his backyard so "I can get some extra work in," he told radio host Dan Patrick.[8] Even the famously reticent New England Patriots coach Bill Belichick came out of his shell to tell me, in a voice from the bottom of a dry well, that what makes a Super Bowl ring valuable, what gives it meaning, is that "it's nothing you can buy, or get lucky and win."[9]

Few athletes have been more deceptively nonchalant in their demeanor than Sampras, a slouchy, gangly lazybones-seeming kid who flapped and shuffled around in slide sandals when he wasn't on the tennis court. In fact, Sampras's game was the result of a tense ambition and implacably self-denying habits. He had an inherently slack build that he spent hours sweating to strengthen with weights and resistance cables in a sweltering Florida garage in the dead of summer heat, because "they don't air-condition the court at the U.S. Open." Even eating was a part of the job to him, a nightly mechanical loading of sauceless pasta, whether he wanted it or, "*choking* it down," he said, because he believed that for him, real excellence couldn't co-exist with self-indulgence. "The truth? You can't have it both ways," he said once.[10]

On the opposite end of the spectrum, one of the most interesting transfigurations was that of Andre Agassi, who turned himself from a peroxided teenager who resembled an exotic little bird, to a burly shaved down man. "What color is your hair, really?" I once asked a very young Agassi.[11] He unhesitatingly lifted his blond tail and revealed the dark underneath, a reflexive honesty that would save him in the years ahead. Agassi was determined to find some authenticity amid massive endorsement campaigns and expectations that "scared" him, he admitted, with their invitation to become a purely superficial creature whose achievements did not meet his wealth. He overcame a powerful combination of pressure and pampering as a child prodigy to emerge a champion of supreme "professionalism." Which he defined as "how to bring out the best when maybe you don't feel like it's there."[12] His splendid comeback and rise to No. 1 is proof that we can redefine ourselves even in midstream with acts of sheer will.

Agassi's resolve to make a better man out of himself took him to some extremes. He had a habit of driving his Hummer into the Nevada desert hills alone at night, to think, or blowing off steam by racing up and down the dunes. One night during an assignment for *Sports Illustrated* magazine, Agassi invited me to go with him, a breath-snatching experience as he jounced over rocks and sand ditches with headlights flickering. But then the ride abruptly ended. The vehicle lurched to a stop partway up a steep incline. Agassi shoved the gearshift back and forth, but the Hummer just shuddered and wouldn't budge. It was stuck. Somehow, in the middle of the desert, Agassi had improbably impaled the undercarriage of the car on a steel pipe jutting out of the sand.

I waited for a sign of petulance, or for him to call a limo. Instead, in a triumph of good attitude, Agassi began to laugh—at himself, at the victory of the desert over his luxury vehicle, and at the sheer unlikeliness of hitting that pipe in the dark. "What are the *odds*?!" he crowed, almost excitedly. Then, with a gentlemanly reassurance, he left me with his cell phone for safety, and hiked off into the dark to find help, heading for some distant headlights. He returned a short while later with a guy in a truck who gave us a ride back into town. Later, as we ate a fine Italian dinner, he kept marveling over the improbability of hitting that pipe. "Do you realize," he asked, "what you've been a part of?"[13]

I do. Across the years, I've attended ten Olympic Games, and almost as many Super Bowls, assorted NCAA Final Fours, bowl games, major championships in tennis and golf, and the odd car race. My appreciation for the actors and their actions in those events has only grown, not diminished. There is too much false conflating of courage with sports competition, but still, the willingness to keep score and say, "That's the best I can do," is a kind of minor bravery, one that demands an interior victory over certain fears and inhibitions. To observe coaches and athletes grapple with these is endlessly revelatory.

"Real sports is not for kids," my father once said. What he meant was, games are more impactful than people might realize. They aren't the gravest endeavor in the world—he loathed excessive solemnity—but they nevertheless contain some serious business. The longer I watch, the more I return to a question my father liked to pose rhetorically. "Who can describe the athletic heart?" he asked. The way he said it made me feel that it was the most important challenge in the world. The following is an effort to answer that challenge—to try to catalog the inner qualities that allow ordinary people to overcome pressures, elevate their performances, and find champion identities, even when they don't always win. In reading, you may decide an athletic heart is worth acquiring for yourself.

1.

The "Right" Call

Decisions under Pressure

Stand with Kansas City Chiefs coach Andy Reid on the sideline, January 19, 2020. His team trails by 10–0 to the Tennessee Titans with a trip to the Super Bowl at stake. The men on the field exhale in plumes, and the crowd noise is a steady rumble from seventy-six thousand fans pulsing distractingly in their team colors of aorta red, as they wait for Reid to make a call. The tension mounts as the last strip of sun sinks over the stadium rim into the cold dusk. Through it all, Reid calmly studies a laminated play card, like he's the only unanxious one in the arena. Like he's sharpening a pencil.[1]

Reid has a decision to make. It's fourth down, with two yards to go, on the Titans' twenty-eight-yard line. The nature of football is that the pressure ratchets on every sequential play. A team has just four tries to move ten yards, or the other team takes possession of the ball. Thus, the calculus alters, and so does the pressure.

Reid has two options, with different magnitudes of risk. He can opt to have his team kick a three-point field goal, which is safe and reliable. But it's also a concession that leaves a taste like cold oatmeal. Or he can go for it, try to punch the other team in the gut with a play that will keep the drive alive for a touchdown and the greater reward of seven points. The praise or blame for what happens next will fall squarely on Reid, and his decision will be perceived as a measure of his courage, recklessness, wisdom, and personality all at once.

Most people are uncomfortable making decisions.

Anyone who doubts this has never tried to choose a coat of plain white paint for a wall. Easy, you think? Perform an experiment: Pick out a can of "atrium" white. See what happens. How could that be a wrong choice? Yet with the first brush, the wall takes on the faint blue tone of antifreeze. Which is fine if you want to live inside an iceberg. Other varieties of white paint yield tints from butter to beige, as you try dove whites, bone whites, Scottish mists, and Acadia moons. At this point, palms slickening with sweat, you may say to your spouse, "*You* try it." Or you might break down and consult a designer, who will say, after listening to your problem, "Oh, the whites are always the hardest."

In fact, picking a coat of paint can be an absurdly stressful experience. It's stressful for three reasons. One, you lack basic knowledge about white paints. Two, you're not especially interested in or patient with matching paints. Three, you're worried about how you'll live with it if you're wrong.

Discomfort and anxiety multiply with the potential consequences of a decision. What doctor to see? What job to take? What amount of debt to risk? What town to move to? Decision-making became even more fraught in the global pandemic. Everyday judgments that used to be easy—whether to eat in a restaurant or travel for a holiday—were suddenly forehead-creasing calculations with costs that could bury you.

The fact is, a lot of us are not especially adept at dealing with life-altering decisions. When they do arise, we greet them with a sense of uneasiness, and struggle to make them. Sometimes we make calls from the "gut." Sometimes we defer to others. And sometimes we freeze, and let events decide us.

"A lot of times, we don't really put together the best game plan for ourselves," seven-time Super Bowl–winning quarterback Tom Brady has observed. "We kind of wake up every day and are very reactive to the situations that happen in our life and you end up never really gaining ground on what's important."[2]

But sport demands decision-making with a special intensity. Each actor on a field of play makes literally thousands of decisions over the course of a game. Some of them are bold and stomach-churning choices and some of them are fractional-second reactions, but all of them are made with the knowledge that their "rightness" or "wrongness" may at a minimum make it hard to sleep that night, and at a maximum could alter futures.

With that in mind, rejoin Andy Reid on the sidelines—and on the cusp of a decision—at that Chiefs and Titans game. He is at a juncture in his career that might give a man pause. He's sixty-two years old, and he knows what it is to be fired. He's got a record of 13-14 in the NFL playoffs, and back in 2012 the Philadelphia Eagles relieved him of head coaching duties over his failure to win a championship.

The Chiefs could badly use some momentum. They are tantalizingly close to a first down—they just need two more yards. But that very closeness complicates things. Fourth down and "short" situations (meaning less than three yards) are torturously problematic statistically. According to NFL data analytics, if coaches would "go for it" on fourth and short more often they would be rewarded with a higher probability of victory.[3] But the sheer fluidity of the game, variables of player behavior and reactiveness, can make fool's gold out of probabilities.[4] Coaches balk, and with good reason. Men are not data. They can fail to execute. This uncertainty can immobilize a coach, and so can fear of repercussions from critics. Kicking a field goal might not maximize Reid's chance of winning a game, but "it could actually maximize his chance of keeping a job," observes the NFL's chief of data Michael J. Lopez, a professor of statistics at Skidmore College.[5]

As former NFL coach Bill Cowher has remarked, "There is so much more involved with the game than just sitting there, looking at the numbers, and saying, 'Okay these are my percentages, then I'm going to do it this way,' because that one time it doesn't work could cost your team a football game, and that's the thing a head coach has to live with."[6]

Suppose Reid declines to kick the three-point field goal and then fails to get the first down? What if three points is the final margin of defeat? What might people say?

Most formal studies of leadership suffer from a fundamental weakness: you can't watch a CEO in live action. Men and women in suits sit sequestered in hermetically sealed towers making deliberations that are largely invisible. They are absent from us. They sweat, to be sure. But they and their experiences are not especially accessible.

Only rarely do we glimpse their process. In the classic business textbook *The Functions of the Executive*, author Chester I. Barnard explained this dilemma: "Not the least of the difficulties of appraising the relative merits of executives lies in the fact that there is little direct opportunity to observe the essential operations. . . . They must be largely inferred . . . from symptomatic indications of roundabout character."[7]

Coaches and playmakers make decisions in real time, right before our eyes. "Quick ones, hard ones," says former Duke football coach David Cutcliffe. "Decisions, that's where the magic is."[8] It's their entire craft. What seem like split-second reactions by even the most impulsive-seeming champions are really micro-decisions, the result of years of trial-and-error assessments, about when to take a shot, if to take it, how to find the opening for it. They not only make calls constantly; they also have the vital ability to persuade others to execute those decisions with similar energy and conviction. In fact, an essential part of their job is the relaying of their vision to their proxies. They bridge the gap between abstract leadership study and practical application. How coaches and athletes act under the stresses of competition can show us how to become more skilled at enacting deliberate, intentional action in our own spheres.

A ball flies through the air, hands are outstretched, the clock ticks, the audience gasps, and careers can be made or broken. Yet athletes and coaches manage to not be paralyzed by those consequences. They decide and they act. It's a breathtakingly instructive thing to watch.

Somehow Reid cuts through it all: the noise of the crowd, the potential consequences for his career. He makes the call. He murmurs into a headset, and suddenly everything shifts into organized flights. Reid and the Chiefs are going for the first down—and with an audacious play. Though they need just two yards, Reid signals a pass. Quarterback Patrick Mahomes rears back and delivers a rope line of a ball toward tight end Travis Kelce.

Two defenders close fast on Kelce. He catches it—they hit him. He holds on.

First down.

The Chiefs go on to score a touchdown and cut the lead to 10–7. Which triggers a complete reversal in the momentum, and the mood in the stadium. By the time the clock expires, the Chiefs have a comfortable 35–24 victory, to earn a trip to the Super Bowl.

After the game Reid muses on that crucial fourth-down play. It got his team "going in the right direction," he says. Asked if the call was a difficult one, he answers simply and succinctly:

"No, it wasn't," he says.

It *wasn't?*

It wasn't. Not for him. Because he knew what he was doing, and why.

We, too, can learn how to make the "right call" under pressure. All of us face uncertainty in our work lives. We report for duty every day in our neckties, work boots, or heels, to face unknown and unlooked-for challenges, problems of "novelty, complexity and open-endedness," as the renowned management-studies academic Henry Mintzberg observes. Still, we show up. That itself is a decision, and not always an easy one. [9]

Though we're hardly aware of it, we, too, make scores of choices every day. Athletes and coaches show us how to drag ourselves from this semiconscious state into more explicit purpose.

What constitutes a good decision? Mintzberg defines it as the ability to sort through "dynamic and shifting factors to make a specific commitment to action."[10] As Mintzberg points out, there are many different types of decisions, from "opportunity" decisions to "crisis" decisions. Just as Andy Reid's predicaments change depending on the down, our own situations vary and so do the stakes. Simply categorizing decisions with more awareness helps us make better ones, and arrive at solid, self-aware, and adaptable judgments amid tremendous uncertainties.[11]

Elite performers are highly methodical in their processes, precisely because they deal in fluid situations. Consistent champions don't just drift through the circumstances of their day; everything they do is deliberate. What you come to notice is that they share some commonalities in how they go about their business, across all endeavors. There is a reason why NFL Hall of Famer Peyton Manning is as good at television as he was at quarterbacking.

"Decision-making is a mechanism, and it can be trained like anything else," big wave surfer and innovator-entrepreneur Laird Hamilton contends. "It's like a muscle, where the more you do it, the better you get at it. And part of being good might just be your willingness to make a decision at all."[12]

These are the elements of a good process for anyone who wants to choose and act well in the face of extraordinary pressures:

- Conditioning
- Practice
- Discipline
- Candor
- Culture
- Failure
- Intention

These elements form a strong chain of causality, and each will be explored in its own chapter. They are fundamentals. A common observation from playmakers is that there is a tendency to need-lessly convolute what creates high performance, to make it seem sophisticated. It's not. "We complicate the formula," says former NFL coach turned broadcaster Tony Dungy.[13] Surfer Hamilton concurs. "We love to disguise imperfection with complication. There is a formulaic process that is very simple, and how you do the little things is how you do the big ones. But people make up real complicated ways to say it. If it's hard to understand, that's because it's babble."[14]

What follows is an effort to cut out the babble.

CONDITIONING

The worst calls or mistakes on the field happen when someone is tired. Marshaling your energies therefore matters. "How you re-spond when you're completely gassed is a big part of making a de-cision under stress," says NFL coach Frank Reich. "What stresses you? Your body stresses you when you're tired. So, you have to pay the price, to know what that feels like, and be able to still perform at a high level."[15]

Laymen tend to think of athletic conditioning as something you do purely to build muscle. But a mountain of neuroscience shows that physical training increases gray matter in the frontal lobes of the brain, enhancing working memory, attention, focus, and executive function, the processes that form basic cognition.[16] Athletes like Michael Phelps don't need to read that neuroscience; they *live* it.

PRACTICE

What made Andy Reid so sure of that fourth-down call? What was his secret to taming uncertainty under pressure? Inspiration? Instinct? Actually, it was something far more banal: rehearsal.

Reid could make that call confidently with the Super Bowl at stake for one reason only—because he knew that it had been so well practiced by his players. Without that assurance, even the best-designed play can make a shot caller look like a fool. "Pressure," Peyton Manning likes to say, paraphrasing the legendary Pittsburgh Steelers coach Chuck Noll, "is something that you feel when you don't know what the hell to do."[17]

DISCIPLINE

How is anyone supposed to know what to do if you're never quite sure what you'll get from yourself, or from others? The elites establish what constitutes good form in any action and work at maintaining it.

Even when they make snap decisions in a fast-moving context, good shot callers are *always married to discipline*. Though it may sound counterintuitive, discipline is actually what allows for effective improvisation—without it you're just an uncontrolled hacker or jacker. If you ever hear a young talent say they want to play on "instinct," you can mark them down as a probable bust. "Not good," says Manning. "It's like saying you don't want to prepare for a speech, you just want to talk from the heart, and an hour later you've said nothing."[18]

Managerial tyrants misinterpret discipline as demandingness. But it's as much about restraint—what you won't do—as what you will do. "Conviction is a good thing, but if you don't have the maturity to know when to exercise that conviction, then you're just a loose cannon," says Reich. ". . . There has to be discretion. If you don't have that, if you make too many decisions without discretion, you disqualify yourself as a decision-maker."[19]

The greats make level-headed choices based on structured habits laid down long before they reach the critical moment.

CANDOR

One virtue all great play callers and playmakers possess is frankness. They have no use for yes-men and -women. None. They are candid with themselves and one another. They certainly have egos, but they have a fundamental lack of vanity when it comes to dissecting their performances, because it's the only route to true assessment.

In the work that any of us do, our situational awareness is limited. It's impossible to perceive all that's going on around us, to know what we've missed, where we were wrong or mistaken. That requires an external critique—if you can take it.

"You can consider yourself a person of high standards *in general* and still have debilitating blind spots," Amazon chairman Jeff Bezos has observed. "There can be whole arenas of endeavor where you may not even know that your standards are low or nonexistent, and certainly not world class. It's critical to be open to that likelihood."[20]

The greatest performers restlessly seek fresh eyes who will point out what they've lost sight of. Nobody ever met her blind spots with a more open spirit of inquiry than Martina Navratilova. In 1989, she felt lost as a player. She had always been a serve and volleyer of tremendous power, but she fell into predictable patterns, suffered losses to lesser players, and went two years without a Grand Slam title. Navratilova went to Billie Jean King and asked her for coaching help. King began by demanding Navratilova explain her own strokes technically, one by one, forehand, backhand, serve, volley. Baffled, Navratilova said, "But you're supposed to teach me."

King said, "I need to find out what you know and don't know."

"But I don't know where to start," Navratilova said.

"Why don't you start with which end of the racket you hold?" King suggested.

After several weeks of fundamental stroke re-analysis, Navratilova was a reorganized player, and a renewed one. She won her ninth Wimbledon without losing a set.[21]

CULTURE

No one succeeds alone, not even a LeBron James. We all live and move within organizations, melting pots in which lots of disparate, highly individualistic, and sometimes egotistical talents collaborate in our successes and failures. Some entities make good decisions more consistently than others for years at a time. Why? What makes a "winning" culture?

We know one when we see one—in sports we call it a dynasty; in innovation we might call it a genius cluster—but we don't often get real insight into how it's really built, because "culture" is such a broad term that its exact meaning is hard to tease out. As Golden State Warriors coach Steve Kerr will explain in this chapter, a winning culture is organically grown, as much as manufactured. What can be said definitively about culture is that certain specific conditions encourage that growth. And the foremost of those conditions is authentic commitment—to the group goal, to your colleagues, to the project, over commitment to yourself.

INTENTION

Pia Nilsson and Lynn Marriott, who have coached four No. 1 golfers in the world, see it on the links all the time: a weekend player decides to try to hit a long iron shot over a lake and fade it to a flagstick tucked around a corner. "Have you ever hit that shot before?" they will ask. "No," is the answer. The weekender doesn't play much golf except on his or her day off. So, what does the weekender do? Tense up, swing fast and hard—and hit it in the water.

Which is an outcome you have no right to complain about if your intention was just to have fun on a Saturday at the golf course. But if your aim was to score better, then it's not fine, and will cause embarrassment and frustration. Too often, we're unclear about what we're really after and what's required to get there.

Many of us bring the same confusion to larger decisions in our lives; we lack a solid picture of what we're doing and why or how much we care about it. *Why did I agree to that?* We're not even sure. Was it to please ourselves, or to please others? Was it to make money or satisfy some other ambition?

"A lot of people don't know, they don't really know, what their core values are, and haven't done the work to dig down deep and look at themselves with some awareness of all that," says Marriott. "There are skills to decision-making, but the foundation has to be your vision and your values. These are superimportant building blocks to know if something is a yes or a no."[22]

What sustains play callers and playmakers amid reversals is their knowledge of why they said yes or no to something. When you know your why, it dramatically affects the definition of success, and your tolerance for setback.

FAILURE

A conspicuous through line among people who perform well under pressure is their acquaintance with failure and the extent to which it shaped them. In fact, they universally describe it as an essential precondition for success. Only through their failures—if they assess them candidly—do they acquire the self-understanding and intentionality that leads to eventual victories and, more importantly, the acceptance of those outcomes they can't control.

Coaches and athletes work in highly visible professions in which there is very little job security, and as Andy Reid can attest, they are subject to fierce external judgment and a high job turnover rate. Every year in the NFL since the 2000 season, an average of seven head coaches out of thirty-two have been fired, almost a quarter of the profession, annually. There is a lot to learn from them about surviving professional pain with buoyancy.

The fact is, it's impossible to fully learn a profession without making mistakes and surviving career reversals. In 1998, Peyton Manning was an interception-prone rookie with the Indianapolis Colts. In a game against the New England Patriots, he played disastrously, throwing three interceptions and giving up a fumble. Manning was so awful that midway through the fourth quarter he thought his coaches might pull him from the game. But they weren't having it—they sent Manning right back in. The lesson was, "No, you stay in there and you figure out how not to throw the fourth interception," Manning says. He responded by leading the team on a touchdown drive. "You could call it a meaningless touchdown," Manning says. "But maybe not. Because it could have gone the other way. It was like, 'All right, I suck. Am I going to go out and throw a fourth interception?' No. Instead, I'm going to try to do some of the things I've learned." It was a critical step in his fledgling career.[23]

Great performers aren't born fully formed and complete. Not only are the achievers included here the products of toil and experience, but many of them came from extremely modest origins. Laird Hamilton was a high school dropout who did construction to finance his surfing before he found a way to make money at his passion for riding big waves in wilding oceans. Michael Phelps's mother was a middle school principal, his father a state trooper. Pat Summitt thought she would be a country schoolteacher.

They acquired their senses of executive command through concentration, preparation, organization, and above all a belief in the improving effects of competition.

If one person impacts these contents more than any other, it's the late great Summitt, the University of Tennessee basketball coach who won 1,098 victories to set an NCAA Division I record for victories, male or female, before her death from Alzheimer's disease in 2018. A close friend and collaborator on three books over nearly twenty years, Pat generously allowed for lurking behind-the-scenes observance.

Pat made a lot of great calls, tough calls, and the main insight she provided was that making those calls can be agonizingly difficult for the unaccustomed. "Most people don't like pulling triggers," she once told me. When I asked her why she thought that was, she replied, "They're afraid of going all in.'"

What stands out most about Pat, all these years later, is that she was unafraid to go all in. And she took sole responsibility for her choices. I never once heard her blame anyone else for the final score.

Watching Pat up close taught that it takes deeply learned experiential skills to lead teams and people to the right headings. It sparked the desire to articulate, as clearly as possible, what separates a person with these acquired skills from the legions of pretenders, imitators, or toxic executives who create so much workplace misery and frustration, and who never seem to learn how to lead or succeed, no matter how many seminars they attend.

A chief characteristic of the high performers in these pages, one identifiable personal quality they *all* possess, is this: they care more about the overall endeavor than their status. They're not overly preoccupied by their fortune or elevation. Make no mistake, great champions can be flamboyant, strong characters. But first and foremost, they lose themselves in the enterprise. They're wholly engaged in the work for its own sake. The riches or fame they might enjoy is purely a secondary consequence.

"Leadership is about other people," Seattle Seahawks coach Pete Carroll has said. ". . . And without that connection there *is* no leadership."[24]

Coaches and playmakers are not the only selfless leaders in the world, of course. As Harvard's basketball coach Tommy Amaker points out, "You don't have to look far to see great examples of leadership. You don't have to seek out some Fortune 500 CEO or amazing athletic coach. There are probably examples of good leaders and deciders in your own household, or in your school. All you have to do is really look and pay attention."[25] But the great benefit of watching the "perspiring arts," as the late great sportswriter Blackie Sherrod called them, is that they are such compelling and immediate dramas and the action is unscripted. They are, as former NFL quarterback Steve Young says, "the greatest human behavior laboratory. The truth happens right in front of you."[26]

If these successful shot callers share a coherent set of learned principles, most importantly they amount to a way of being. A principle is not a management ploy or a stratagem, or a maxim, or a ruse. Those things won't prevail over instability. Principles are foundational modes of behavior. They permit men and women to make hard and even undesirable choices without panic and with the clear-eyed recognition that though we might be at the mercy of unpredictable forces, we can at least employ sound practices and over time increase our odds of being right, more often than not.

2.

Conditioning

The Body

For twenty years, Michael Phelps swam for five miles a day, six and seven days a week, trawling through resistant liquid, staring at a black line on the pool bottom. Phelps swam on Sundays, and his birthdays. "Nobody else did that," his coach Bob Bowman says. When Phelps's chest began to bloom with gold medals, outside observers attributed it to a genetic gift. But that missed the most important fact about Phelps, one with significance for all of us. "The thing that made him great was the work," Bowman observed.[1]

One afternoon during a bus ride to a competition with some fellow Olympians, another swimmer asked Phelps a question.

"You train a lot, don't you?" the swimmer asked.

"I guess," Phelps said.

"But you don't train on Christmas Day, right?"

"Yeah, I do," Phelps said.[2]

It's a consistent misunderstanding of great achievers that they come preloaded with some unattainable gift, some farfetched, advantageous anatomical quality. *Scientific American* even tried to assess whether there was some freakish, unusual proportionality in Phelps's six-foot-four physique that set him apart. In fact, besides just slightly long arms, Phelps's measurements fell within predictable ranges for his height. "It couldn't just be that the guy trained his guts out," an exasperated sports medicine expert told the magazine.[3]

This is a point too many people miss in their day-in and day-out. Anyone who wants to be consistently excellent at their living must have a more-than-passing acquaintance with conditioning, even those who suppose they work purely above their necks. The tempo of demands in the twenty-first century have made conditioning a growing requirement—and a topic of inquiry—among great deciders in all realms. Analysts at the *McKinsey Quarterly* have recognized "the connection between physical health, emotional health, and judgement." Those who ignore it will find themselves trailing in a wake—just as Phelps's competitors did.[4]

By 2008, Phelps was an international force, fully in his prime, and he set his sights on an all-time Olympic record. Phelps wanted to go for eight gold medals at the Beijing Games. No one had ever won more than seven in a single Olympic meet, a mark set by Mark Spitz in Munich in 1972. The record had stood for almost four decades.

To break it, Phelps would have to swim in seventeen races in just nine days between qualifying heats and finals. It was a daunting prospect. Swimming is a uniquely exhausting trial: it takes every muscle in the body to move through the water, which is twelve times more resistant than air. The exertion is so taxing that a long day of training might burn around ten thousand calories. The Beijing attempt would put an almost-inconceivable strain on Phelps's body—but it would also challenge his mind.

He was likely to face the closest races of his life, when he was most tired. Phelps and Bowman therefore knew that they would have to condition him as much mentally as physically.

Without the ability to think and gauge alertly in the moment, he'd be just another disappointed man who had an ambition but couldn't quite carry it out.

The brain robs your body of the energy to think. Just because you're sitting in a chair reading or typing, barely lifting your arms above desk level, doesn't mean you aren't physically working. You are, quite strenuously, especially after three or four hours of sustained thought. Even in a resting state, it's estimated the brain consumes about 20 percent of the body's fuel.[5]

Disney chairman Bob Iger, at seventy years old, has the physique of a mountaineer. He rises at 4:15 every morning and does forty-five minutes on a VersaClimber, a torturous cardio machine that mimics rock-climbing. Three times a week he couples it with weights, and three other days a week he adds a twenty-five-mile bike ride, and at the end of every evening he walks another three to four miles.

"In reality, in the job I have, you're working just about every moment that you're awake, and under those circumstances you have to protect yourself to maintain your mental and physical health," Iger observes. "My workouts are designed to make sure I'm in top physical condition, and I do it for sanity, too. I find it is a head clearing."[6]

Condition literally means the working order of something, its state and quality. A wealth of neuroscience shows that exercise—strenuous movement—improves the quality of your mind by enlarging and stimulating certain reactive areas in the higher order regions of the brain that govern evaluative thought. The transfer of metabolic energy literally lights these areas up, exciting neuronal signals, creating synaptic plasticity, and allowing for faster processing of information. The allure of watching great athletes lies in their full realization of the capabilities inside their skin, not just of their bone and tendon. Any longtime observer of them can't fail to notice there is a glow to them, a vitality. We are all creatures of light and electricity as well as tissue, and exercise acts within us like stirring of a swarm of fireflies. It creates a fundamental emergent energy, one we are all capable of tapping—and the more we have of it, the more vivid our thoughts are liable to be.

Exercise engages powerful systems throughout the body that work in concert: the pumping of blood, oxygen, proteins, and other nutrients creates mitochondria, known as "the powerhouse" of the cells, which charge human biochemical physical reactions as well as facilitate neuronal activity. One neuroscientist has compared mitochondria to the battery-pack arrays that Tesla sports cars run on.[7]

All of this has an impact on the dynamism you bring to a specific task, whether mental or physical. The energy required for problem-solving is enormous. Imagine how hard the brain must work so that synapses can organize the otherwise stupefying onrush of sight and sound you experience in a single moment.[8] The brain is never switched off; even at night it's sending blinking electrical signals. It's responsible for the biggest portion of the power bill that comes due in your body and it needs continual recharging. Where does it get the recharge? Partly from movement.[9]

Merely rising from a chair and walking feeds the brain, almost like a windmill or waterwheel. This powerful feedback cycle was explored in a May 2018 study that showed how load-bearing leg exercise helped to grow healthy new nerve cells in the brains of mice. This is perhaps one reason why mental decline can be so dramatic in people who suffer from muscular diseases that atrophy their legs. [10]

Researchers at Cambridge University in England used elite rowers to explore this co-dependent loop. They recruited sixty-two students from the university's oar crews to perform a combination of mental and physical tasks. First the rowers did a three-minute word recall test. Then they did a three-minute power test on a rowing machine. Lastly, they did word recall *while* rowing at maximal output. When they tried to remember the words while gasping for breath, their *physical* drop was far larger than the mental one. Their strength scores dropped by a third, 29.8 percent, compared to their mental scores. Chief author Daniel Longman concluded that there was an "acute level trade-off": When skeletal muscles competed with the brain for available glucose and oxygen, they lost. Big-time. The brain ruthlessly plundered the body in order to think efficiently.[11]

Now think again about Michael Phelps as he churns through the water and consider what is happening beneath his skin and scalp. Imagine the magnificent neural swirl and loop, from body to brain and back again, that his strokes create.

Phelps was lucky to fall under the tutelage of a coach, Bowman, who grasped this neuroscience and knew the effect of those seven-days-a-week laps was far more pervasive than merely training sinews. Bowman had an eclectic mix of expertise: he majored in classical music and minored in psychology as a swimmer at Florida State, and he brought both of those experiences to tutoring Phelps in how to perform under pressure. He wanted the swimmer to be like a pianist, who practices measures on a piano until they are so memorized that he can *play* a piece with feeling—and do so even under a bout of nerves while performing in public.

When Bowman first noticed Phelps, he was a promising but thrashing kid in the pool at the North Baltimore Aquatic Club. Bowman sat him down and explained that he could be a potential Olympian, but it would depend not on what he did in front of a crowd on race day but on his willingness to do laps when no one was watching on a Wednesday morning. Conditioning "is about building an infrastructure," Bowman says. "What we were doing on these laps in the early years, we're trying to build a physiological structure that will hold up to the stresses he's going to face down the road."[12]

When people are fatigued the first thing that suffers is form. During those innumerable laps, Bowman's aim was to groove Phelps's strokes so that he could sustain the right rhythm and body placements as he sculled through the water, no matter how exhausted.

"I think the hardest thing to do, the hardest time to do something, is when you're tired," Phelps told me during a midwinter conversation in Bowman's small office just off a pool deck at the peak of his career. Phelps had agreed to sit for a multimedia *Washington Post* project with the intriguing title "The Psychology of Speed." Open on a desk in front of him was a training notebook. "I have one hundred and seventy more days of this," Phelps said, pointing at it. "Brutal." But it was worth it, he said, for what it gave him in the heat of competition: he knew that his strokes would hold up better than his rivals' over the last abdominal-torching few meters.

"When you're tired it's just sort of easy to fall apart," Phelps observed. "Over the years in the workouts, when Bob's gotten me to the point where I just can't move, he's demanded of me that I still do the *right* turns, the *right* stroke. So that once I do get to that stress level, I can still handle everything the right way and how I need to."[13]

At the root level of confident decision-making is reliability. It's not enough to decide what you want to do; you have to be able to command your body to *do* it. Athletes achieve this command through adaptation. When you impose a new challenge or workload on yourself that you have trouble meeting, the stressful sensations intersect at the emotional center of your brain—which reacts by directing your system to upgrade itself, so it doesn't have to feel uncomfortable anymore. As you repeat and reinforce, your responses under the duress become more consistent.[14] As one influential Russian trainer has observed, the right conditioning for a task creates a "harmonious unity" that allows *all* of your responses to fire on command in coordination, "psychic, technical and tactical."[15]

Bowman overloaded Phelps with multiple swims in a day, seeking this upgrade. Phelps would tell Bowman, "I'm so tired." Bowman would reply, "Let's do just one more. Let's see what you got in you." There were times when Phelps balked at swimming so many events and wanted to skip a race. Bowman said to Phelps, "*No.* You don't want to be the person who gave up when it got hard."

Three times a week they did double workouts, cold early morning endurance swims followed by technical workouts in the afternoon, fine-tuning his strokes. There were lung-searing trips to Colorado Springs to train at altitude for days at a time, not just because altitude would boost his lung capacity but because "how to do your best in an environment that might be unpredictable or harsh, and how to win a race by a touch, they go hand in hand," Bowman believed.[16]

Phelps and Bowman began setting milestones in conditioning to see if Phelps could reach them. Phelps would strive for a world-best time on a particular stroke and distance—and then Bowman would say, "Let's do five straight repeats of it, just to nail it." The records began to fall.

As they approached the Beijing Games, Phelps was reaching his physical and mental peak, with rope-thick skeins of muscle and a chest blown wide. Just as important, he was an utterly fluid performer. He had made the almost-musical neurological shift Bowman had long sought, from racing as a conscious operation to a free, unconscious performance. Phelps just knew where he was in the pool, how close or far from the wall, from the rhythm of his stroke. Bowman's musical training had completely taken hold of him; he was like a musician who had internalized whole measures of a piece.

Phelps didn't operate on conscious thought, any more than a pianist focused on individual notes, which would slow down the piece. Yet while Phelps was unthinking, he was sharply perceptual. He had an intense awareness of everything in and around the pool, especially any competitors who might creep up on him out of the corner of his eye. He was so hyperalert that sometimes Bowman was astonished by it. The North Baltimore Aquatic pool had a broad open deck with glass lobby doors at one end. Once, Phelps finished swimming his laps and bobbed up and said, "Did my mom just walk into the lobby?" In fact, she had.

Phelps reinforced his conditioning with a totally unvarying, consistent routine at every race meet. Phelps and Bowman would arrive at the pool precisely two hours early. Phelps would do a series of warm-up exercises, the same ones he'd been doing since he was eleven years old. Bowman wanted it to be "automated," and as calming as a mantra.

By the time Phelps took off from the starting block, he went like a clock, churning through the water as if he had a mechanical gear train. His pace had become "second nature," he said. If he followed Bowman's careful programming—if he did so many fifty-meter laps at just the right pace and nailed the numbers five times in a row—he *knew* he was ready to win. "And then it was my job to just sort of let it happen," Phelps said.[17]

But just a few months before Beijing, a disruption nearly ruined all that careful, methodical work. After leaving the pool one day, Phelps slipped and fell in an icy parking lot and fractured his right wrist. The doctor looked at his chart and said, "Hmmm, you're a swimmer?"

Yes, Phelps answered.

"Well, this is a pretty big fuckup then," the doctor said.

Phelps needed surgery and would be out of the pool for at least two weeks, the doctor said. Even when he got back in the water, he'd be restricted to kicking only while his wrist fully healed.

Phelps was inconsolable. "I just gave away three or four gold medals," he told Bowman. The Beijing record seemed unattainable without being able to condition. "It's over; it's finished," Phelps said.

But Bowman assured him the record was still possible, given the underlying fitness Phelps had developed over all those years of training. To maintain it while he was restricted to dry land, Phelps rode a stationary bike for three hours a day. Once back in the water, he did hundreds of yards of leg-only laps with a kickboard, further strengthening his already massive legs and lower-body mechanics. He emerged from these sessions with an even more powerful surge.

The challenge in Beijing was not just how to physically manage so many races in so few days. It was also a question of whether Phelps could manage his emotional energies through a bedlam of distractions and pressures. From the Opening Ceremonies onwards there would be a crush of media attention on him, interrogations from the press amid blasts of klieg lights, a clamor for his attention from commercial endorsers, all of it potentially draining. Other swimmers would be only too happy to take advantage of even the smallest lapse.

The body-brain loop works both ways. Just as physical conditioning shores up the brain's performance, the reverse can also be true: a mental drain can impact muscular endurance. One study of Italian soccer players showed that doing fatiguing brain teasers before going to the practice field made them commit more errors in controlling and passing the ball. Another study of twenty-one young boxers showed that too much time on phones playing video games affected their speed reactions in the ring.[18]

Bowman therefore tried to toughen Phelps's mind to deal with factors that would tax him mentally. It was great that Phelps had such a deeply embedded inner clock—but what would happen if that timing failed or was disrupted by all the distractions? "What if things don't go well?" Bowman suggested. He asked Phelps to envision a series of distressing situations. What if he *trailed* on a final lap? How would he respond if his goggles came off? Or his suit ripped?

Bowman and Phelps worked through potential scenarios using visualization. Phelps would imagine a setback, and swim it out in his head. He thought about "how I *don't* want the race to go" and then saw himself turning it around.[19]

It all counted. Phelps would need every measure of fitness, every ounce of anticipation, every cellular-molecular reaction, in Beijing. Early in the Games, one of those things that *could* happen *did* happen. In the two-hundred-meter butterfly, Phelps's goggles leaked. They flooded with water until he couldn't see the wall. He stayed calm, relied on his rhythm, and won pulling away, though with bloodshot eyes. "I was *ready* for my goggles to fill up with water," he said later, gratefully.[20]

For much of the rest of the competition, Phelps looked like he would power through. He won six gold medals without another hitch. He set a new world record in the most difficult event, the two-hundred-medley, a muscle-flaming race that demanded all four strokes: the butterfly, breast, backstroke, and freestyle.

But that's when it happened, the moment they had conditioned for. As Phelps touched the wall and bobbed out of the water, he was too fatigued to even throw his arms in the air. Bowman noticed his lack of celebration, watched his expression carefully, and thought, *Oh my God, he's so tired.*

It was a bad moment to crash. Phelps was scheduled to swim a semifinal in the one-hundred-meter butterfly in half an hour.

Bowman hurried to the mixed zone, the area where competitors warm down, and found his swimmer. "I don't have anything left," Phelps announced.

"Well, you better fake it, because you've got this semifinal in twenty-two minutes," Bowman said.

Somehow, Phelps got through the heat. But walking down the back hallway afterwards, he said, "Bob, this is the most tired I've ever been. I don't know if I can do it." Bowman insisted that he could. Phelps had the stamina and neurological firepower, but he also should have gotten something more from all the conditioning, Bowman told him. It should have bred conviction, the knowledge he had outworked everybody and *deserved* to win.

"You know you can do it," Bowman said. "Just act like *you*."[21]

The one-hundred-meter butterfly was Phelps's final individual event. If he could somehow win it, he would be all but assured of breaking Spitz's record. There would be nothing left after that but a team relay, in which the Americans were heavily favored.

As Phelps took the block for the butterfly, he told himself to treat it as "a normal race, I'm in my normal spot, in the middle of the pool."[22]

But it wasn't a normal race, or a normal spot. The gold medal record was on the line. And next to him in Lane 4 was Milorad Cavic of Serbia—the reigning European champion and a blisteringly fast swimmer. Also, a fresh one. Cavic was so set on beating Phelps and preventing him from setting the record that he had withdrawn from another event, the one-hundred-freestyle, to be ready. Meanwhile Phelps was swimming in his sixteenth race of the meet.

Cavic was renowned for opening fast—and away he went. Phelps knew he had to stay within half a body length of him to have a chance. If he got too far behind, he'd get a wave in his face, and it would be over. As long as Phelps could see Cavic from the corner of his eye, he knew he was in striking distance. Still, Cavic was ahead. Phelps delivered a powerful turn kick and started chasing. When he felt the heavy splashes from Cavic's own effort, he knew he had drawn alongside him.

The final wall loomed. But Phelps realized his rhythm was slightly off. His last stroke wasn't enough to get him all the way there—his unfurling body was already slowing. He had a fraction of a moment to make a tactical decision.

He could continue his long glide path and hope to out-touch Cavic. Or he could take one more shortened half stroke—and try to chop the wall, as it's called in swimming. The drawback to a chop is that the recoil of the water off the wall can actually cost a swimmer fractions. The wall was so close. . . .

Cavic was gliding.

Phelps decided. He convulsed his shoulders and unleashed a last plunging half stroke. Both men reached out, Cavic, fully outstretched and skimming, fingertips seeking, Phelps thrashing.

Phelps all but slammed headfirst into the wall.

Briefly, he thought he had lost the race. He came up for air, sucking in huge inhalations with his mouth in a large, "Ohhhhhh." He jerked off his goggles to look at the board and heard the roar.

Phelps: 50.58.

Cavic: 50.59.

Phelps had won—by one one-hundredth of a second.

Phelps drove a fist overhead, and then slapped the water with his palms, throwing up fountaining geysers of water. He had tied Mark Spitz's gold-medal record.

After the race, Bowman met his swimmer in a back hallway.

"Well, you cut that one kind of close," he joked.

"I know," Phelps said, grinning.

A day later, Phelps had his record eighth gold medal around his neck when the American team won the relay. Seventeen races in nine days, sometimes with just minutes between them, world records and fatigued leg-dragging heats, had come down to that one-hundredth of a second in the butterfly, and a single decision. The chop was exactly the right call.

"I guess the speed and the tempo of it was perfect," Phelps said later, sitting in Bowman's office. "I guess, you know, for so many years I've done so many small things that have helped."[23]

To Bowman, it was simple. It had been, Bowman said, "a conditioned response."[24]

If you're offered $500 now, but you can have $1,000 by waiting three months, which do you take? The quick cash or more money later? The answer to that question says something about your ability to compete with a Michael Phelps. Because he will wait. And then he will wait some more. He will give up today's fun for tomorrow's reward, and eventually he will bury you with all the loose change that is the difference between his willpower and your itch for immediate gratification.

The behavioral-science term for the inability to resist immediate gratification is "delayed-reward discounting." Some people tend to perceive something as less valuable the longer they'll have to wait and work for it, discounting its worth. Whereas others are stronger at seeing and attaining more distant-horizon goals. Willpower is "one of the most relevant predictors" of long-term professional success, according to behavioral health researcher Michael Sofis of the firm Advocates for Human Potential. If that discourages you, here's the good news: evidence suggests you can enhance willpower with physical conditioning, cultivate it.[25]

The filmmaker Stanley Kubrick was a famous chess addict who competed for cash at the boards in Washington Square Park in New York City before he became an auteur with a camera. Asked once why he found the game so entrancing, he answered, "It trains you to think before grabbing." He expanded on this thought with a description of delayed-reward discounting that would please any behavioral scientist.

"You sit at the board and suddenly your heart leaps," Kubrick continued. "Your hand trembles to pick up the piece and move it.

But what chess teaches you is that you must sit there calmly and think about whether it's really a good idea and whether there are other better ideas."[26]

The ability to resist impulsivity is, of course, a key facet of strategic decision-making. And don't kid yourself: resistance is hard. In fact, it can be as hard as working on all cylinders, and just as enervating.

You can see this in the heart rates of world champion chess players, whose heart rates can triple to cantering under their shirts even as they project a lethal stillness over the board. The impression of supreme chill has earned world No. 1 Magnus Carlsen the nickname the Dalai Lama of Chess. Not coincidentally, Carlsen is as sculpted as a pro athlete, thanks to a regimen developed for him at Norway's Olympic training center. He showed off his physique when he turned up late for an internet-online match in his boxer shorts. Social media commentators dubbed it "The Shirtless Gambit."[27]

Anyone who doubts that strategic thought at a desk requires stamina should consider that top chess players lose ten pounds or more in tournament play, with a metabolic burn rate approaching six thousand calories a day, as ESPN documented in a piece titled "The Grand Master Diet: How to Lose Weight While Barely Moving." In 1984, Anatoly Karpov dropped twenty-two pounds during his siege-like five-month World Championship standoff with Garry Kasparov. Stanford evolutionary neuroscientist Robert Sapolsky has suggested that chess grandmasters undergo physiological stresses similar to those in competitive distance running.[28]

In 1975, a pair of American researchers named Charlotte Leedy and Leroy Dubeck wired tournament chess players with sensors to study their physiological responses during the hard thought of competition. Breath rates tripled. Adrenaline surged.

Pulses galloped; muscles contracted. And in some cases, systolic blood pressure skyrocketed to over 200. All while they sat virtually unmoving.[29]

"Your body has to be in top condition," the legendary Bobby Fischer once remarked. "Your chess deteriorates as your body does. You can't separate body from mind."[30]

Fitness tracking has become a game within a game at modern chess tournaments, as rubbernecking audiences watch for clues of mental cracking and physical distress in quirky, contemplative figures hunched over the boards. At the 2018 Isle of Man International Chess Tournament, metrics projected on a large screen revealed that grandmaster Mikhail Antipov torched 560 calories sitting stock-still for two hours. By way of comparison, the average person will only burn 100 calories running a mile on a treadmill.[31]

The champion at this game within a game is Carlsen, a phenom who became the world's top player in 2010 at the age of nineteen. In a stunt at a tech trade show in Vegas in 2014, Carlsen beat twenty inferior competitors simultaneously, all of them wired with heart monitors. Their heart rates hopped along at a pace of 139 beats per minute. Carlsen was so unthreatened by the contest that his barely pattered at 70.[32]

But the game is hardly effortless for Carlsen, as another tech exhibition revealed when he met the famed American chess and Twitch prodigy Hikaru Nakamura in a match outside of Oslo. Both wore Polar bracelets. Late in the match with a time limit looming, Carlsen made a miscalculation and a poor move—and his heart rate checked in at a jogger's 129.[33]

Carlsen's recognition that conditioning is vital to his judgment at the chessboard led him to visit the Olympic training center in Oslo in 2017. He was still just in his mid-twenties, but the stress of defending his status as the world's regnant player had begun to tell on him, and he felt himself faltering in the final stretches of five-hour matches. The Olympic performance consultants suggested he give up his habit of drinking an orange juice during a match—it was causing him sugar crashes—and recommended a new exercise and nutrition regime. Carlsen began to train for tournaments with high-intensity interval workouts of thirty to sixty minutes on treadmills, hot yoga, and several hours of competitive soccer, tennis, and basketball weekly.

"Games are lost or won in the final hours due to mistakes caused by fatigue," he told the *Wall Street Journal*. On another occasion he said, "It's vital that I feel good in my body if I'm going to be in complete control of my faculties."[34]

Chess above all is a game of delayed gratification: as players struggle for control of the board they also fight to subdue their desires and egos, as they decipher feints, sacrifice pieces, and evaluate the wisdom of varying attacks. They have to check their impulses and, as Kubrick put it, "think about whether it's really a good idea and whether there are other better ideas."

To Sofis, it's not surprising that chess players would find that physical conditioning enhances their judgment and decisional restraint. As the head researcher in a group of scientists at the University of Kansas, he demonstrated that it was possible for almost anyone to improve their willpower by using exercise.

Sofis and his colleagues recruited sixteen volunteers of varying ages with sedentary habits to undergo seven-week individualized walking-jogging programs. Before, during, and after the seven-week regimens, the subjects took a standardized twenty-seven-item question test called the Monetary Choice Questionnaire. The test is geared to evaluate someone's delay-discounting willpower. The findings were published in the journal *Behavior Modification*. Thirteen of the sixteen participants showed markedly more self-control in financial decisions at the end of their training. Not only that; the effect was lasting. They *kept* their greater self-control in follow-up testing fully a month afterwards.

Why did the physical regimen work? Because, according to Sofis, exercise acts on willpower as a "self-control future valuation multiplier that can spill over into decisions in other areas of your life." When you make yourself exercise consistently, it improves mood, reduces stress, and enhances cognition—which then reinforces your desire to repeat the healthy activity. Your willpower accrues like interest in bank account. "We are faced with these little decision trials many times each day," Sofis says. "And sometimes the delayed reward is months or even years removed, but each choice is impacted by previous ones and impacts future ones."[35]

What Sofis discovered in a clinical experiment former New York Yankees head of performance Dana Cavalea can verify from his experience cross-training executives. Cavalea has established a flourishing sideline working with CEOs who realize they need to be to "fit to win"—not fit in the sense of a pro athlete, but simply responsibly fit, solid enough in their bodies and habits to play the long game and make sound decisions for themselves and others. Cavalea has met dozens of get-rich-quickers with high short-term yields and Cohibas in their fists, who folded like "human houses of cards" and lost their positions or businesses because they had high impulsivity and lousy eating habits. He likes to quote former Yankees equipment manager Rob Cucuzza, who would watch a flash-in-the-pan batter and say, "He's hot right now, but let's see who he really is in the next three months."[36]

Cavalea points out, "I don't care who you are today if you can't be that same person tomorrow." The habits that workaholics think show commitment—fast-food binges, short sleep, overstimulation from multiple pinging devices—in fact, make for erratic performance. They shatter attention and make one prone to instant gratification. All of which can provoke one to grab before thinking, as Kubrick would say.

Followers don't trust impulsivity—they view it as weakness, and they are right to. Impulsivity is linked to everything from overeating, to gambling, to substance abuse. Nobody is inclined to enthusiastically enact a decision from someone who looks or sounds dissolute. When researchers from the Center for Creative Leadership cataloged the habits of 757 upper-management American executives over a five-year period, they found the most successful ones tended to exercise more and smoked and drank less on average than their peers. What's more, their colleagues *perceived them as more competent*. An aura of fitness affected their projections of authority.[37]

Everyone can learn from the athletic mindset how to be better conditioned and a less impetuous or rash decider. Like Magnus Carlsen, we're all required to perform sitting down for five and six hours at a stretch and know the peculiar exhaustion that can come from that posture. It's the most common experience in an office. And yet we still have to find a calm competency and make good choices. Conditioning can allow you to play that chess game.

Stress is what happens when you face a demand that you aren't conditioned to comfortably handle. If you're not accustomed to driving a race car at 200 mph and then suddenly try to occupy that driver's seat, you won't have the resources to meet the moment. The gap between the demands of the situation and your capacity to deal with it will cause you to tense, your perceptions will blur under the onrush of stimulus, and you will likely panic. But with conditioning, you can acclimate to the speed and stressors of the situation.

Stress gets a bad name. Most people mistakenly associate it with purely negative effects, with *dis*tress. It actually serves a fundamental purpose in human physiology: the discharge of cortisol, and the speeding up of our heart rates and shortness of breath that come with the fight-or-flight response may feel like ill effects, but they're also signs that your body is producing energy and getting more oxygen to your brain to push you to full wide-awakeness. Stress-response is your biochemistry's way of helping you "rise to a moment that matters," argues health psychologist and Stanford Business School management-science professor Kelly McGonigal, author of a book entitled *The Upside of Stress*, who lectures on how to "make stress your friend."

Try an experiment: The next time you're on your bike riding downhill, let it go faster—not to the point of real danger, but to the point of intensifying the experience until it makes you a little nervous. Watch your own reaction to it. You will likely find that it makes you hyperaware and focused on the road in front of you. Pushing yourself to an uncomfortable point is important, because the triggered emotional and chemical reactions that come with stress "produce alertness," big wave surfer Laird Hamilton says. "And we're meant to experience that."

Hamilton has spent his adult life exploring profound stresses and making close friends with them. He has sat on a board in the midst of liquid vastness, waiting for a massive wall of breaking water in remote seas where the shore was just a thin horizon line. What he has learned from studying large waves is that almost any stress can be managed with enough conditioning to it. The most famously dangerous ride of his life took place in 2000 at the hurling Teahupoo reef off Tahiti, a break so menacing that the cover of

Surfer magazine showed him in a blue barrel of centrifugal reversion, with a murderous ledge over his head and the headline *"Oh My God . . ."* But Hamilton had spent years educating himself to Teahupoo's particular hydraulics.

Surfing a large wave is an experience of full-body intensities and yet requires a kind of inner stillness—and that stillness can only be acquired by multiple forms of conditioning—including conditioning for *fear*. Beneath most compromised decision-making in any field is inexperience-driven anxiety, Hamilton believes, and that can be mitigated with systematic exposure, by "getting to the walls of discomfort and dealing with that discomfort, getting comfortable with being uncomfortable," Hamilton says.[38]

Some of what Hamilton has done is so risky that no one else had ever tried it before. How do you condition for the outermost brink of fear? There was no template to conditioning for one-hundred-foot waves, so he had to invent one. One pillar of his conditioning, Hamilton decided, had to be consistency. Large swells do not particularly follow schedules—he had to be mind and body–capable of riding the unlooked-for rogue wave. Hamilton invented his own routine, based on his anecdotal knowledge of oceans.

He studied breathing techniques employed by Navy SEALs, and the Dutch extreme athlete Wim Hof, nicknamed the Iceman for his serenity in harsh conditions, to learn to self-calm and build longer breath under crushing white water. He studied how ancient Polynesians trained for coping with heavy seas by moving large rocks underwater, and devised a pool-bottom workout that involved crawling forward while dragging weights, to increase his tolerance for long stays beneath the surface under duress.

The result was an innovative conditioning and breath-work program that he now exports to a range of high-performers out of his home in Malibu, from actors to NBA players. Called Extreme Performance Training (XPT), it's based on Hamilton's simple conviction, instilled by his experiences on the ocean, that the ability to acclimatize is one of "the most powerful human traits." And unlike other celebrity training regimens, it incorporates a significant emphasis on stress, fear, and anxiety.

Make no mistake, Hamilton is still fearful in the ocean. He's taken at least a thousand stitches. Once, the point of a board hit him in the face and left a puncture wound in his cheek, and on another occasion a fall on a big wave separated his ribs from his spinal column. He has been temporarily lost at sea. He's been pushed thirty feet down into the black with his feet strapped to a board.

But over the years Hamilton has also been anxious in everyday situations—like giving a presentation to business executives who might not respect a surfer. The body under stress doesn't necessarily recognize what it's being stressed by, Hamilton realized. He might be stressed because his daughter took the keys to the car and she was very late getting home. Or he might be stressed because he couldn't see the shore. The two brands of anxiety basically feel the same.

Which has led him to toy with simple ways to condition for more common brands of uncomfortableness. One is exposure to ice and heat. Hot and cold are intense neurological experiences, hard to bear for long without a sense of alarm. Hamilton began to subject himself to intense temperatures for a few minutes at a time via ice baths and extended high-heat saunas. The body, Hamilton decided, was a good teacher when it came to stress.

I want to get out.

But you're not going to get out.

I want to get out.

No, you're going to stay.

Eventually he would succumb and get out. "But just the process of having that exposure and forcing your body in that stressful position, it makes you deal with any kind of stress better," he says.

Hamilton's ideas track those of academic stress investigators. Research scientist Firdaus S. Dhabhar has experimented with using short bursts of intense exercise to trigger positive chemical stress responses that can enhance the body's vaccination and immunotherapy reactions. When the body fires up its multiple powerful physiological systems—from cardiovascular to muscular-skeletal and neuroendocrine—it also releases some of the substances that nature gave us to help the body fight infection. Ice and heat work to decrease pain in joints and tissues, for instance, by provoking anti-inflammatory reactions and cell repair. If you can learn to bear these sensations better and even greet them as not unwelcome, use them right, they can be healing.[39]

Few people realize it, but along with cortisol another stress hormone is released, a neuropeptide: oxytocin. One of oxytocin's roles is to help heart cells regenerate—it actually strengthens your heart. "Mastery of challenges is protective," McGonigal has observed. [40]

Most of us sedentary professionals don't pay much attention to our personal chemical responses to events. Instead, in the face of stress we often turn to stimulants—especially sportswriters. Coca-Colas. Coffee. Sugared drinks. The trouble with any stimulant is that it doesn't last long enough to help you in sustained thinking. Short-term jolts actually exhaust you. Athletes and chess players don't drink a Coke and eat a donut before a contest, because they know they'll crater. But deskbound decision-makers do the equivalent all the time and then wonder why we are so mentally tired, and irascible, and make poor choices.

In sports, that lack of priority on conditioning and reliance on stimulants will get you cut, traded, or fired. What real competitors across all spectrums know about conditioning, whether chess players or race-car drivers or surfers, is that it's the essential separator between them and spectators. The willingness to undergo hard conditioning—to marshal their physical and mental resources in an organized way to meet discomfort—is the difference maker between those who compete over a long career and those who flame out. It's what gives them professional resilience.

Most people will never experience what it is to swim nine thousand yards with an Olympic gold medal in mind. Or to ride a wave that looks, sounds, and feels like a mountain collapsing underneath your feet. But everyone knows what it is to try to make an important life decision under tension, with a rising sense of anxiety. Conditioning is really just an instrument of human learning, and it's not only elite athletes who can gain from it, Hamilton points out. "It's the rest of us who have the most room to grow," he says.

3.

Practice

The Mind

The great conjurer Ricky Jay once said that what makes magic is practice. Sleight-of-hand artists can only vanish a coin if they've perfected the technique by rolling it over their knuckles thousands of times. Ricky Jay's definition of a true magician, therefore, was not someone who stood on a stage with trunks and puffs of smoke, but rather someone so well rehearsed they could "stand a few inches from you and with a borrowed coin, a lemon, a knife, a tumbler, or a pack of cards, convince you he performs miracles."[1]

Practice differs from conditioning: it's strategic, informed, targeted work, usually under the evaluative eye of a teacher or coach. Though the two can have some overlap, conditioning is about broad development of capacities, whereas practice is about refinement of skills through diagnosis and rehearsal. The word "practice" evokes tedium, but it's really a matter of being interested in and willing to work at critical details. This vague yet fundamental misunderstanding results in a lot of bad or ineffectual practice: work without meaningful results.

Good practice is transformative. It's what converts any ambition or dream into physical reality. It's an essential component of the right call under pressure, for the simple reason that if you can't count on a certain level of skilled technical precision from yourself and the people around you, your strategic choices will be limited and you will be, frankly, nervous. "Confidence drops when technique is weak," Billie Jean King once declared. When you've practiced exhaustively, your options will be more open, your doubts fewer, and your choices more sure and perhaps bolder. It's easier to go all-in when you know what you have to give.[2]

"I'm a big believer in practice until you can't get it wrong, whether its sports or business," says the NBA's Dallas Mavericks owner Mark Cuban. "If you have seen the circumstances, be it a deal, or a play unfold in sports, then you can recognize it quickly, respond, and decisively make the decision of what to do next. It all comes down to preparation."[3]

The "wet ball" practice drill seemed silly to the 2006 Indianapolis Colts. They played in a dome, for God's sake, that never let any rain in. Still, at least once every other week, the Colts coaches led by Tony Dungy would spray the footballs with water until the leather turned slick and dark. They'd make Peyton Manning and his center Jeff Saturday practice with them, work themselves into a full lather meticulously rehearsing how to safely exchange a wet ball from the center to the quarterback, at game speed, on their trickiest plays. "Why are we doing this when we play in a dome?" Saturday would ask. Manning would shrug and joke, "Jeff, there could be a leak."

They made it to the Super Bowl that year, which was scheduled to be played in Miami, outdoors. Normally, February is the dry season in Miami. What's more, no Super Bowl had ever been visited by rain. Yet on the day of the game, Manning looked out of his hotel window and what did he see? A virtual monsoon, sheets of unseasonable rain blowing sideways. Manning knew instantly that he had an advantage because he'd practiced so often with a slick football. The Colts would not have to limit their game plan to their most conservative plays. He felt a flood of relief that Dungy had insisted on getting out the hose at those practice sessions, to prepare for the rare eventuality. He said to Saturday, "That's why we've been doing all those wet balls for the last few years."

Almost an inch of rain fell that Sunday, with winds gusting to 20 mph. During the halftime show producers were terrified that Prince would slip on the soaked Formica stage as he rocked the world with an exuberant rendition of "Purple Rain" amid the downpour. But Manning and the Colts never had trouble handling the ball—every exchange he took was a safe and confident one. Meanwhile their opponents, the Chicago Bears, twice fumbled the ball away on snaps to quarterback Rex Grossman. Turnovers were a major difference in the game, as the Colts went on to a 29–17 victory.

"It was a perfect example of preparation to avoid feeling pressure," Manning recalls. "Pressure would be to wake up in Miami for the Super Bowl and it's raining and you say, 'Oh my gosh, it's going to be wet; I'm not sure I can get the snaps from Jeff.' I left the field a lot of times saying I wish I could have had a play over again, or a series over again. But I never left the field saying that I thought I could have done more to *get ready* for the game. And that always gave me peace of mind at night."[4]

As the great basketball coach John Wooden once observed, "Don't mistake activity for achievement: practice the right way."[5] So what constitutes the right kind of practice for a particular endeavor? First of all, your practice must have a purpose, a sure understanding of what the point of it is. Second, it should have measurable results.

Few entities are a more interesting study in good organizational practice than a great NFL team, and few are more reliant on it for even minimal competence. Each franchise operates amid inherent instability. The roster of fifty-three players changes seasonally; new talents are signed, and old ones retire—the average career span of a player is just 3.3 years. Injuries mean the team's makeup can change weekly, with substitutes stepping in and player combinations constantly reshuffled. Familiarity with co-workers is ever in flux. Then there are the demands of planning for different opponents.

"There's so many people that have to be coordinated," Tom Brady observed during a corporate Q&A appearance for Adobe in 2020. "In a way it's like an orchestra, you know, there are so many people who are so unique and have such different skill sets, such different responsibilities, and when it's done right it's really magical. But it's *hard* to do right, because you got your opponent trying to force you to do everything wrong."[6]

NFLers are therefore necessarily expert in developing highly structured "practice plans." Their week begins with a fundamental question: What to practice? Since it's not possible to practice everything all at once, what's the most important immediate goal? Then, once you decide what to practice, *how much* to practice it? What's the right input to achieve a result, without overworking to the point of diminishing returns? The answers to these questions coalesce into the "game plan," designed by the head coach, which is essentially the overall conceptual battle plan aimed at that week's opponent. Contained within it are the practice priorities, the emphasis points of rehearsal.

Game-planning was heavily influenced by the great NFL Hall of Fame coach Bill Walsh, who once observed, "The less thinking people have to do under adverse circumstances, the better. When you're under pressure, the mind can play tricks on you." Walsh didn't show it much outwardly—he was a cool, erudite figure in a headset during his run of three Super Bowl titles with the San Francisco 49ers in the 1980s—but he hated the strain he felt when searching for answers late in games. He wanted "to remove from a tough situation the panic element of 'What the hell are we going to do now?'" he wrote.[7]

The success of all great NFL play callers and decision-makers thus begins long before the game ever starts, days and even weeks before kickoff. They seek to exploit the laxity of their rivals with detailed analysis and practice, and not just any kind of practice, but rigorous work toward identifiable goals, improvements.

"The lucky thing in sports is that at the end of the week we get to determine how well we planned, how well we practiced, and then ultimately how well we played," Brady told the Adobe Q&A audience. "The problem is, if you plan wrong and evaluate what you practiced wrong, then when you get to the competition you're already starting out behind another team or competitor that may do things the right way. So, you've got to make sure you got the right processes in place."[8]

For twenty years, nobody in the NFL practiced better than Brady and the New England Patriots. From 2001 to 2019, the Patriots were the untouched masters of "execution" under pressure as they reached nine Super Bowls and won six of them. "Execution" is a term too often used as a bland, meaningless generality. What it means is a precision-blade, mechanistic excellence, achieved through drill and rehearsal. Everyone preaches execution. But few were able to imitate the Patriots' standard of it, which at times appeared, well, magical:

Twelve times in playoff games, Brady led the Patriots on winning drives in the last minute or overtime. Somehow he conjured come-from-behind victories out of what seemed like losing circumstances with almost no time left. That's twice as many comebacks as any other quarterback in league history.

This was not the result of improvisation. It was a matter of synchronized action based on work from Monday to Friday. Expert observers who watched the Patriots over that 2001–2019 span all agreed: they practiced in a way that separated them from other good teams. In 2014, the rising young head coach of the Los Angeles Rams, Sean McVay, had a chance to watch the Patriots practice in a joint off-season workout. He would not forget the impression they left on him: keenness in every drill. There was never an idle or apathetic movement, even at the most minor-seeming tasks. "If you knew nothing about football—not a thing—and you just watched them, you'd say, 'There's something different about that team,'" McVay told NBC's Peter King.

McVay walked away from the practice thinking, "That's what it looks like when it's done right."[9]

Anyone who got a glimpse inside the Patriots' home stadium would see Belichick and staccato-shouting assistant coaches continually cleaning up slippage in the most nuanced skills of the most well-paid veterans. Players worked on techniques until they were ingrained deep into their bones. Hand position, foot placements, precisely how to bat down a pass, how to shed an opponent's grasp, or gain physical leverage on him. "There was no number on it until we got it right," recalled Lawyer Milloy, an All-Pro defensive back who spent eight seasons there.[10]

Nothing that might become an inflection point in a big game was too small for the Patriots to practice. They even rehearsed exactly how to hand the ball to the referee between plays during the last two minutes of a contest. It's a habit in the league for players to casually toss the ball to the ref after a play. But if the ref doesn't catch it, it goes bouncing around on the turf, wasting a precious second. The Patriots were drilled to sprint to the ref and hand it to him to save half a tick. And they would "go over and over and over it," according to former player Reggie Wayne.[11]

It was dubbed "the Patriot Way," as if it was a kind of dogma. Belichick became an infamous personification of it, with his hoodie sweatshirts cut off at the sleeves and his terse, workman-like answers during press conferences. But the Patriot Way was actually just about conscientious habits and Belichick's simple mantra, "Do your job." It was his belief that most organizations beat themselves, rather than got beat. During an interview for the *Washington Post*, I asked Belichick to summarize his philosophy. This was his reply:

"If you can't execute what you're trying to do in practice, you're not going to be successful," he said. "You've got to have good fundamentals. The No. 1 thing is unforced errors. It doesn't matter who you're playing. They don't even have to be out there. If you can't do things properly without resistance from an opponent, you're in trouble. Start with that. Once you eliminate things like penalties, turnovers, mental errors, you know, you just go out there, and get a play called, and run it the way you're supposed to run it. Until then—until you can do that—there's not much of a chance to win."[12]

The Patriots' run of appearing in nine Super Bowls over twenty years had one hallmark above all others: they played stunningly mistake-free football. And that was due to the demands of Belichick, whose mania for practice was such that he would rather go with a lesser player who performed well every day than a more talented star who might oscillate and cause uncertainty. He wanted players who were "dependables," he told Suzy Welch of CNBC. "You have to go with the person who you have the most confidence in, the most consistent. . . . I'm going down with that person," he said.[13]

In December of 2009, Belichick sent four players home because they arrived for practice ten minutes late in a heavy New England snowstorm.[14] "You want to be able to trust that guy playing next to you, and behind you, and he has to trust you," Belichick once observed. And trust was built in practice. "It's day after day, after day, after day, after day."[15]

Most NFL coaches quiz their players every week to see how well they've absorbed the game plan. But Belichick went one better. He would assign younger players to write essays about whom they'd would be facing and what their quirks were, down to their personal tics. And then his players would go out and practice against those specific qualities. As a rookie, Milloy was assigned to research a tight end for the Green Bay Packers. "I had to talk about where he was from, what college, who his mom and dad were, how many siblings he had, whether he was married, what was his favorite food, what was his best route, and how fast he was," Milloy recalled. "A complete evaluation. Not just his name and number. It was that detail oriented." The idea was that if he ate with his right hand, then force him left.[16]

The Patriots' meticulousness was joined with a physicalness in practice few other teams were willing to risk. Most teams practice against a "scout" team, a squad of reserve players, to ward against injury. But the Patriots sometimes used their starters against their starters to get ready for critical contests. "We wanted them to see what it was really going to look like in a game," remembered defensive captain Willie McGinest. "We would give them a *full-speed* look." When commentator Phil Simms observed a Patriots practice just before the 2016 AFC Championship Game against the Pittsburgh Steelers, he was "shocked" at the fierceness of the workout. Brady and receiver Julian Edelman began screaming at each other over a mistimed pass. They beat the Steelers, 36–17.[17]

The result of all that practice was indeed measurable. During their run, the Patriots committed fewer penalties than any other team in the league. In seventeen playoff games between 2011 and 2017 they were whistled for infractions at a 25 percent lower rate than their opponents. Think about that. When it came to game-killing mistakes, they were fully one-quarter better than their opponents. You only achieve that by practicing the most banal things cleanly to the point of perfectionism.[18]

Another measurable: they almost never gave the ball away. There were no cheap gifts to the opponent, hardly a dropped handoff or botched interception. Yet they excelled at forcing the other team to cough it up with mistakes. From 2001 to 2019, the Patriots had the fewest giveaways of the ball in the league, while also leading the league in takeaways. This was worth a thousand points—literally. Over that decade they scored 1,013 points off of other teams' mistakes. That's a staggering difference maker.[19]

The sheer consistency of the Patriots' execution put pressure on opponents before a game ever began. Manning was one of the few quarterbacks to experience much success against them—he led the Indianapolis Colts and Denver Broncos to Super Bowl titles in 2006 and 2015 partly at their expense. Yet even he remarked on how mentally difficult it was to get ready to play them. "They were just so sound, in a Football 101 kind of way," Manning says. "We'd say, 'We have got to be equally as disciplined and fundamentally sound.' They just didn't 'bust' a lot." "Bust" as in make a critical error that ruined their synchronization. One of the things this soundness meant was that Belichick endured a lot fewer difficult, behind-the-eight-ball decisions.[20]

Still, the Patriots run couldn't last forever. It was just too arduous to sustain. Between playoff games and Super Bowls they played the equivalent of a full season more than any other team in the ten years from 2010 to 2020. Fatigue and mental staleness eventually set in. Belichick's voice wore thin with Brady, who at the age of forty-three moved to Tampa Bay, seeking fresh energy and a sunny new environment. (And by exporting his practice habits, Brady promptly helped make a champion out of a team that hadn't been to the playoffs in a decade.)

Yet to this day it's hard to find a better case study of the efficacy of "practice" than the Patriots, and of how it could elevate seemingly ordinary players to great heights. The Patriots never had the strongest roster in the league—and, in fact, often had supposedly glaring deficits at certain positions—because they consistently eschewed expensive stars for the sake of dependability and payroll integrity. Their 2005 Super Bowl team, for instance, had thirty-nine players who were either undrafted or drafted in the third round or lower. "Chip guys," as Brady called them, meaning chips on their shoulders.

Receiver Julian Edelman, one of those undrafteds, began to understand the ethos in the locker room in his second year as a pro. Late one night he came out of the facility's treatment room, after doing an ice bath for an injury. Though it was nearly midnight, the famously forbidding Belichick was in the training room watching film—while stalking on a treadmill—and preparing for the next day's practice.

"Coach, you sure like football, huh?" Edelman said.

Belichick answered, "Beats being a plumber. See you tomorrow."

Edelman told the story at a press conference to accept the 2019 Super Bowl Most Valuable Player Award. Sitting next to him, Belichick just smiled and said, "I have a ton of respect for plumbers."[21]

The difference between elites and amateurs is that elites practice those things they are worst at and dislike the most, while the rest of us run around our backhands our whole lives, or live with a weak left hand, or avoid doing math. Public tennis courts and golf courses are full of people who inherited some natural physical ease, or were gifted a few expensive lessons, yet have never learned to cure their worst swings.

As individuals, athletes are as flawed as you or me, of course. But as performers, they know something the rest of us don't: the value of remedying weaknesses instead of just playing to your strengths. When you don't mitigate a weakness, you limit your available choices of action, and are only playing on half the field or court.

It was always an interesting question what Peyton Manning inherited from his Heisman Trophy–winner father, Archie, and what he acquired for himself. By the time Peyton won a final Super Bowl in 2016 at the age of thirty-seven with a zipper scar on his neck from soldered-together vertebrae, stoop shouldered and slack armed compared to his youth, it was safe to conclude that his inherited genetic gifts were the least of him. Even in shoulder pads he looked lank and relatively unmuscled next to younger specimens, and with his shirt off, well, he was no Gatorade commercial. Yet Manning remained one of the most dangerous competitors in the game to the end of his career because he was its most compulsively meticulous practitioner at those things he did poorly.

On the very first day after a season ended, Manning would meet at 7:00 a.m. with his quarterbacks coach to watch tape—not a highlight reel of his glorious moments, but of every interception he had thrown that year, spliced together on a loop. Manning would study all of his worst moments, each throw that landed in the hands of the opponent, and grade it as either "avoidable" or "unavoidable." An avoidable interception was an undisciplined play where he tried to force a ball deep downfield when a better throw was open. The unavoidables were good throws that hit a receiver in the numbers, but the ball just popped out or the defender made a great play.

When the tape ran out, Manning wasn't done. He would cue up a new tape, this one of all the close-call interceptions that opponents *could* have had from him if they hadn't dropped the ball. He would grade those throws, too. "That's kind of a hidden tape that a lot of people don't get to," he says. Then he'd watch tape of the potential touchdown passes that he had missed, when he *should* have scored but for some reason didn't. "So, it was a humbling start to the off-season," he says.

Manning watched every lousy, failed play, not as an exercise in wincing humiliation, but to see what was correctable. "What we did off that film, was look for commonalities," he says. Patterns, tendencies in his mistakes. The tape might show he had a tendency to throw interceptions when defensive linemen dove at his feet. Nervous feet disrupted his motion. "We would then create a drill to work on that," Manning recalls. He'd practice finishing his throws while coaches threw heavy bags at his cleats.

"There was very much of a process: let's take what we see on film and put it on the field," Manning says. "Otherwise, what are you watching the film for? You better go do something about it on the field."[22]

To what extent practice can make someone world-class, as opposed to fortunate genetics and any other of God's unequally distributed gifts, is a highly disputed topic in the human performance field. But what's not disputed is that the right kind of practice that targets specific weaknesses, whether in hitting a baseball or delivering a presentation, has improving effects and that improvement is available to anybody. Cognitive scientist and president of Barnard College Dr. Sian Leah Beilock says: "Given enough practice and the right mindset, everyone has the potential to excel with regard to pattern recognition and decision making."[23]

"Practice" has been an ill-used term, largely thanks to the popular misconception that ten thousand hours of it is somehow a "magical number." The idea gained wide currency when Malcolm Gladwell tried to define a threshold for achieving "true expertise" in his elegant 2008 bestseller, *Outliers*. But the research Gladwell relied on, authored by human performance psychology scientist K. Anders Ericsson in the 1990s, doesn't actually endorse a specific magic number of hours. Rather, Ericsson was more concerned with the *type* of work required, what he called "*deliberate*" practice—the type of highly analytical practice that Manning engaged in. In 2019 before he died, Ericsson tried to clarify once and for all what he really meant by "deliberate practice," frustrated that his work was oversimplified by those seeking to emphasize the role of genetics in human performance. It was a view he had no use for. "Consistently and overwhelming, the evidence showed that experts are always made, not born," Ericsson wrote.[24]

Most of us engage in what Ericsson called "naïve" practice. We work at a hobby like the guitar until we get pretty good at it, and that's where we stay, on a plateau. But "deliberate" practice focuses on harder, smaller breakthroughs, with the sort of continual assessment Manning did. It consists of using "informative feedback" to engage in "remedial training," Ericsson wrote. The greats cure their most marginal deficits with specific work plans for, say, increasing the agility in their nondominant foot.

Most importantly, they understand that these incremental refinements have immense capacity for growth over a long period of time.

Ericsson pointed to one study that showed that athletes who reached the echelon of international competition spent *eight times* the number of hours in practice under the analytical eye of coaches than athletes who competed only at the state level. In short, most high school jocks were strictly local—perhaps because they believed a little too much that they were "natural" athletes. Meanwhile more modestly "gifted" strivers eventually outstripped them, perhaps by being more conscious of their defects.[25]

Ericsson's ideas matter in decision-making because he homed in on an elemental difference that distinguishes great performers in any field: they're willing to continually examine whether they're as competent at something as they *think* they are. They "uncover misperceptions and faulty assumptions—what they think they know but, in fact, do not," observed Ericsson's friend and fellow researcher Ulrik Juul Christensen. They *look* for their mistakes. Whereas the rest of us are less than fully aware of ours or cover them up.[26]

Tom Brady became great not because he was born with a special gift but because he was willing to accept the harsh verdict that he was not born with one. Even as a mature Super Bowl–winning quarterback he took—and accepted—piercing critique from Belichick in practice. Aqib Talib, a former defender for the Patriots, told this story to ESPN: One day in practice when Brady threw an interception in the middle of the field, Belichick exploded at him in full view of everyone. "You got 130 career interceptions and half of them are on this route. You keep doing the same s—— over and over and this is what happens."[27]

Brady's response was not to brood over the insult, but to seek a fix. Like Manning, every off-season Brady reappraised his performance. Under the eye of a renowned throwing coach named Tom House, Brady sharpened his downfield accuracy by critical percentage points. Brady and House would examine a 3D analysis of his motion frame by frame for any inefficiencies or slippage. In his first decade in the NFL, Brady completed roughly 62 percent of his passes. But from 2014 onwards, Brady would complete at least 64 percent or more of his throws in seven of eight seasons. Brady worked so tirelessly on his throwing motion, was such a perfectionist about it, that on one occasion he refused to autograph a picture that had caught him in a sloppy moment. "Look at my mechanics," he complained. "I can't sign that." In 2021, though he was almost forty-four years of age, he hit 67.45 percent, the second-best accuracy rate of his entire career. Brady even made a late-career adjustment to his shoulder rotation that gave him a few extra rpms of velocity on the ball—which led to a quicker release by seven-tenths of a second.[28]

"What separates these elite athletes, the Hall of Famers, is that they try to get better every day, not by twenty percent, but just one or two percent," House observes.[29]

How many people are willing to practice for just 1 or 2 percent improvement? Peyton Manning and Tom Brady are.

Why does deliberate practice work so powerfully? It's helpful to understand that it has a neurological building-block effect. The brain is improvable. To learn to do anything, whether catch a pass or speak a language, awakens intricate sets of circuits involving motor function and visual-audio processes. As we practice, our brains absorb and internalize information in order to use it more efficiently. The messaging system from thought to action becomes more supple—and reactive—until a truly well-practiced act can make someone seem downright clairvoyant.[30]

Watch the tennis great Rafael Nadal return a 135 mph serve. He crouches and waits, as his opponent tosses the ball in the air. The server lassos the racket—and Nadal is already there to meet the ball, and drives it back at a clean, sharp angle. How is it that he reacts so quickly? Nadal is not extrasensory or possessed of superpowered reflexes. What looks telepathic is really a practiced response to specific physical cues that allows him to be preemptive.

Biomechanical analyses of how top players like Nadal intercept serves have shown that they do not have especially superior reactions to you and me; they simply understand better the path of flight, based on hours of structured, strategic work at their sport. Australian neuroscience researcher Bruce Abernethy showed this with a series of famous "occlusion" experiments.

Abernethy wanted to identify how world-class athletes perceptually process a speeding ball, versus lower-level competitors. He asked tennis players to wear goggles that prevented them from seeing their opponent's service motion. Abernethy found that top players weren't reacting to the ball once struck but rather were highly practiced in visually reading their opponents' bodies—cues novices were not attuned to. The pros responded to the subtlest shift in a shoulder movement that altered the trajectory of a serve, while average players waited until the racket was in motion, costing them reaction time.[31]

In other words, even the most responsive-seeming athlete moves based on experience. As Beilock has explained, "Underneath it is a lot of dirty practice."[32]

NASA relies on the effects of dirty practice perhaps more committedly than any other organization on the face of the earth. Astronauts must perform tasks as if they are second nature, at mortal peril. They ride to work atop an exploding bomb and live for six months at a time on the International Space Station, which is basically a giant fan in the dark sky surrounded by crumpled foil. A spacewalk requires hanging upside down in feet clamps at the end of a robotic arm, swaying like a kite on a string. The heavy suits and the narrow margin for error make working in space such a heart-pounding, pressure-packed exercise that veteran space walker Bob Behnken, former chief of NASA's Astronaut Office, describes it as akin to "a biathlete trying to race from point A to point B, and then stopping and getting a gunshot off at a small target." NASA training therefore focuses intensely on grooving the right courses of action. NASA requires an astronaut to rehearse the smallest job, even turning a bolt, at least eight times—on more complex tasks the ratio is 17–1—*without a single mistake*, hitchlessly, end to end, in an underwater simulator, until it's clear he or she can't improve any more.[33]

Rehearsal for flying NASA's craft is even more demanding. No commander flew the space shuttle without doing over *one thousand* practiced landing approaches. The idea being that even in the most tired and debilitated state after a mission, and regardless of weather and other variables, the pilot's experience of a landing would be so familiar that any last-minute decisions or adjustments are clear, if not automatic. "That well-worn path and muscle memory, and the decision-making, will work," Behnken says, "because they have seen it at least a thousand times before."[34]

Still, sometimes even the most task-fit person can fail at the simplest thing. What happens to *those* circuits between brain and body? How is it that a highly practiced pro athlete can make bonehead mistakes? Take a pro tennis player who double-faults on a big point or a golfer who misses a short putt. Why does an expert break down in performance under pressure?

The answer is that "rarely do we practice under the conditions we actually perform in," neurologist Beilock says.[35] Sounds simple. Makes sense. And yet across professions most of us fail to practice in the actual "game speed" conditions we will be asked to think and perform in.

Beilock cites a common example: We practice for presentations by studying relevant material. But when we have to actually speak before an audience, the book or the file won't be readily available and there will be inquiring eyes appraising us. Even more important, we'll be asked to summon information in *a short amount of time*. Beilock therefore suggests we should make study more stressful. Impose deadlines. Practice quickening your recall by enforcing a time limit on yourself. "In closing the gap between training and competition, you want to practice the things that you have to do when it matters most," she says.[36]

Pressure is not a just state of mind—it has actual physical properties. In fact, the use of "stress" was first employed by the pioneer endocrinologist Hans Selye, who borrowed it from engineering to describe the almost-weighty force of physiological strain he observed in a body's response to adverse events.

When your body shunts blood to large muscle groups in a fight-or-flight response, it simultaneously sends less blood to smaller muscle groups. They're siphoned, drained. So, you lose fine motor control. Your hands and feet quit working as efficiently. A simple task a sportswriter has done her whole life, namely typing, can suddenly feel harder on deadline. That's because it *is* harder. You have less blood in your hands and fingers. Also, it's harder to think. That's because your brain function is altered; as your body tries to help you with heightened alertness, it also narrows your focus, which can create a tightening, tunnel effect. All of this is why a pro tennis player is suddenly so inhibited he or she can't toss the ball straight, or a writer might fumble at the keyboard and transpose letters in simple words.

"Very few people—even adult athletes—realize how our thinking is shaped by the body," says Beilock, author of a definitive book on the subject, entitled *Choke*. "The mind is not a one-way control center that gives the body orders; the body can actually influence the mind."[37]

Beilock's interest in the physiological forces that can foil a well-practiced act comes from a personal experience. In high school she was a soccer goalie with the ambition of making it into the Olympic development program. One afternoon the national team coach came to the field to evaluate potential talent. Beilock was so uptight that she tipped a ball into her own net. As she related in a 2017 TED Talk: "I choked under the pressure of those evaluative eyes on me."[38]

Later, as a cognitive scientist working at a University of Chicago human performance lab, Beilock wanted to get at the root of what makes skilled people misfire when it counts: Where might the short-circuit in choking be? She had a hunch, from her soccer debacle, that it lay in "maladaptive control," a state of performance anxiety that interferes with the subcortical regions of the brain that coordinate skilled task demands. People in a state of maladaptive control try to impose "step-by-step monitoring" on what should be automatic free-flowing procedures. A simpler term for which is "overthinking." Beilock and a team of fellow researchers designed a study in which they asked elite collegiate soccer players to *think* about which side of the foot they were dribbling with as they moved through a set of cones. The players became so excessively mechanical that their footwork suffered measurably compared to their normal performance. In another experiment, Beilock asked experienced golfers to explain their putting stroke step by step, and to identify precisely when their clubhead stopped. Again, their accuracy suffered. Instead of letting their well-practiced strokes come forward, they were so focused on how to govern their limbs that they actually clenched up and became clumsier. "Attending to procedural skills hurts performance," she concluded.[39]

Maladaptive control is essentially an attention-imbalance problem—you're paying too much attention to what should be a relatively unconscious task. The cure is to take some of your attention away, and thus rebalance your neuro-responses. One way to achieve this balance is by distracting yourself with an uncomplicated mental task, like counting, or humming a song, Beilock suggests. As part of her experiments with golfers, Beilock asked them to putt while listening for a series of tones. This time, they were more accurate. They were better putters while thinking about something else than they were while focused on each motion of the putting stroke. Taking some consciousness off the physiological mechanics freed them up, allowing practice to reassert its grooved effects.[40]

Perhaps the best way to think of the well-practiced mind, Beilock suggests, is as a beautifully lit room. Stress can affect the lighting—for better or worse. It can sharpen and enlighten things, or it can be blinding. The trick is to light the mind appropriately for good performance under the circumstances.[41]

Successful athletes and coaches experience just as many sensations of alarm or anxiety in response to challenge as you or me. "Under certain adverse circumstances anyone's mental preparedness can falter," Beilock asserts. But they learn ways to mitigate or reframe their adrenal firings to continue to operate under pressure—and what's fascinating to any sportswriter is how they manage to do it on a regular basis. It's not random and it's not luck. The lesson to take from them is utterly counterintuitive. The essence of their performance is not that they do something extraordinary and extreme under pressure, but rather the opposite. When they are at their best, they are simply performing in their usual ordinary and well-practiced way.

"People think some of us rise up to pressure, when really, what science shows is that it's not that some of us rise up, it's that a lot of others get weighed down," NFL coach Frank Reich says. "The people who are best in the moment don't get weighed down. . . . They have an attitude of, 'I've done this a lot, and if I miss, I miss.'"[42]

Many of us falter in the midst of competitive situations due to a muddled inability to understand what's happening *as breakdowns occur,* and therefore we're unable to stop the cascade of unwanted responses. An old ballplayer's phrase for it is "white line fever." White line fever is what happens when someone steps past the painted sideline on the game field—and into such an emotional-adrenal maelstrom they can't perceive what's going wrong or slow themselves down. "When it comes to mind-body stuff, probably 98 percent of athletes fail because of the inability to match up their thinking and their feelings to what they are being asked to do competitively," observes Brady's throwing coach Tom House, a former major-league pitcher himself who later obtained a doctorate in sport psychology.[43]

Famed agent Leigh Steinberg, who represents Patrick Mahomes, aptly describes the challenge a quarterback faces in the heat of a contest, and it doesn't sound much different from the challenge any one of us faces in an overwhelming day: "He's thrown a couple of interceptions, the game is getting out of hand, the center is looking at him like he's on hallucinogens, and now what does he do? Can he compartmentalize, adopt a quiet mind and elevate his play?" Steinberg asks.[44]

The best quarterbacks can tame themselves because they have the peace of mind that comes from thorough, *ongoing* deliberate practice. They don't just stop when they've made it in the pros or fixed one physical flaw. As Manning and Brady demonstrate, they relentlessly dissect and examine their reactions year after year in a quest for fail-safe mechanics.[45]

Given how long some of this science has been around, why don't more people follow the "deliberate practice" process? For a good reason: it hurts. Not rhetorically, or abstractly, but in actual felt experience.

Rewinding the mental film of a subpar performance like Manning did can be depressing—and surprisingly limb deadening. In 2004, cognitive researchers mapped the brains of Canadian swimmers who had failed in the Olympic trials. The swimmers were asked to watch video replays of the events while undergoing functional magnetic resonance imaging (fMRI) brain scans. As the swimmers relived their career-threatening losses, frame by frame, they showed surges in the parahippocampus center of their brains that signaled deep emotional pain, distress on a level with someone with a serious mood disorder. What's more, they showed *decreased* signaling in the premotor cortex area of the brain, which sparks movement. Their emotional disturbance came with a lethargy in their arms and legs, which affected their desire to get back in the pool and return to practice.

Canadian national team psychologist Hap Davis, who directed the brain-mapping project, decided to try a cognitive intervention. He asked the swimmers to watch their races again, but this time to deconstruct them clinically. In individual twenty-minute sessions, they cataloged the aspects of their swims that had been flawed and identified how they would swim differently in their next race. Once they had self-evaluated, Davis asked them to undergo a new set of brain scans—while watching the footage again.

In these scans, their emotional distress was less pronounced and their premotor cortexes were activated. They wanted to get back in the water.

By analyzing their performances in technical terms with an eye toward what to practice, the swimmers felt primed to swim again. What this told Davis was that when people are left on their own to brood over reversals without help in deliberately unpacking them, it can lead to lassitude, compounded poor performance, or even surrender. The old-school approach of simply haranguing or "chewing out" an athlete for a loss was therefore likely to do more harm than good. The Canadian coaches began doing targeted analytical film sessions with the swimmers, with marked improvements. Davis's work led him to a conclusion that is critical for all of us, whether we're athletes or not. "Resilience is lost with unprocessed failures," he has observed.[46]

The lesson: a single mistake or reversal is *not who you are*. The greats turn self-recrimination into self-analysis and design better practice. Calling yourself a loser, assuming that you are a head case, does nothing. Good practice doesn't eliminate stress altogether or mean you won't ever experience it again. What it does do is give you instruments to manage it, in the face of tensions. "We can learn to overcome the unhelpful knee-jerk reactions and tendency toward defeatism, while developing mental toughness and a determination to persevere in the face of obstacles," Beilock asserts.[47]

An informed understanding of what's happening in a performance gives you a chance to self-correct, if not in the moment, then afterwards with dedicated work. But you can only acquire that understanding with a wholesale awareness of your tendencies, good and bad, under the most difficult scenarios. You don't get better by practicing purely in smooth conditions. And yet it's so tempting.

Golf—perhaps as much as any undertaking—is a welcoming "activity trap" in which practice conditions don't come close to actual play. We stand on perfectly flat driving ranges beating balls into the broad distance, admiring the flight of the ball. But playing a golf course requires hitting shots from a million different uneven positions, awkward side-hill lies, ditches, dirt patches, sand bunkers, or over water. Small wonder then that people suffer such performative collapses on the golf course—and then wonder what happened to their beautifully practiced swing.

One term for this is "unconscious incompetence." The phrase is used by Eric Ericsson's friend and fellow researcher Ulrik Juul Christensen to describe how otherwise accomplished people can be totally unaware of vulnerabilities that lead to failed decisions. Christensen has found that in professions as wide-ranging as academia, medicine, and engineering people are typically "unconsciously incompetent" in 20 to 40 percent of areas "critical to their performance." Example: at a tech company, sales employees didn't truly understand the features of a particular product they sold, ignorant to about 22 percent of its capabilities. And yet they thought they knew everything about it. "Unconscious incompetence can be found at every function, discipline, and level in organizations," Christensen wrote in *Forbes*. "In fact, it's often more prominent among experienced staff, which is particularly problematic because, as the go-to people in their circles, they often pass incorrect or incomplete information and skills on to others via peer-to-peer learning and training. This can lead to significant mistakes."[48]

Golf coaches Pia Nilsson and Lynn Marriott spend most of their time identifying these personal blanks that can lead to emotional landslides when their clients are under pressure. Nilsson and Marriott use a range of techniques to "capture" their players under the strain of actual course play. They ask them to keep journals of exhaustive notes about their routines, what they thought and felt during a round. How did they warm up? What did they say to themselves on a good swing? If they didn't manage a stressful hole well, what were the whispers in their heads?

In the final round of the 2007 Kraft Nabisco Championship, golf pro Suzann Pettersen held a four-shot lead with four holes to play, normally a circumstance that is a near lock for victory. Instead, she disintegrated. The twenty-six-year-old Pettersen lost to an eighteen-year-old named Morgan Pressel. By the seventeenth hole Petterson was so out of sorts that she glanced at the leaderboard and told her caddy, "We're tied." Actually, she still held a one-shot lead. But her vision was so affected by the pressure that she misread the board. She finished in tears.

After taking some time to recover emotionally from the loss,

Pettersen sat down with Nilsson and Marriott to review it. They used videotape for close observation of body language and facial expressions, searching for clues of tensions Pettersen may not have even realized she felt. They identified two distinct physical reactions in Pettersen when she was trying to make a swing decision: she would tense her jaw, and stand over the ball for an unusually long time, overthinking, without being particularly conscious that she did either.

Petterson's tight, frozen jaw would lead to stiffness in her neck and shoulders. The longer she was still over the ball, the worse the stiffness got. By the time she swung, the tightness had radiated throughout her upper body and would ruin her technical motion, making her short-arm the ball at impact.

Nilsson and Marriott explained the effects the stress had on her jaw, neck, and shoulders, and thus her swing. By studying her physical tendencies and cataloging what she felt on each hole, Pettersen recognized where the emotions had first begun to gather, and then cascade. "When you're viewing events from a disassociated position, then you can really clean out the learning," Marriott says.[49]

Two months later, Pettersen led again in a major event, this time the final round of the LPGA Championship. Before she began play that Sunday, Nilsson and Marriott told her, "Most likely those not-so-good tendencies are going to show up again. But you have an advantage now. You know what they are." They had rehearsed ways to keep her jaw and upper body loose. One was with a breathing technique. Another was just to chat and tell silly jokes to her caddy throughout the round. Talking to him lightly kept her jaw from locking up.

It worked. Pettersen found "the calmness where I know I can perform my best." She shot a final-round 67 and held off a charge from seven-time major winner Karrie Webb. She won by one stroke.[50]

The lesson: even the most high-achieving, self-aware professionals need help sorting out their responses and learning how to practice.

All elite coaches and playmakers concur on what constitutes good practice: it's purposeful, prioritized, detailed work that results in a measurable enrichment of skill. It's the only route to what might be called polish, in anything. Through it, good decision-making under pressure becomes smoother and faster, with less hesitation and more dependable results. It's the ultimate paradox: The end result of all that dirty, technical, tiresome rehearsal can be a surpassing grace. Maybe even magic.

4.

Discipline

The Framework

Too many times to count, NBA coach Doc Rivers has seen cell phones get in the way of winning. Rivers tries to discourage players from checking statistics on their phones at halftime, because he doesn't want them fixated on personal scoring. If a guy knows he shot 1-10 in the first half, it might affect his play in the second half; make him overaggressive or, worse, hesitant, and either way ruin the team's flow. Nevertheless, often when Rivers walks into the locker room to address his team at the break, what does he see? A lot of bent heads. Guys are staring down at the devices in their hands, checking their stats online. Not only that, they're reading texts and tweets *about* their stats.[1]

What is Rivers supposed to do? Ban all cell phones? Bench the worst offenders?

Rivers has an aura of authority. He's six-foot-four, the son of a cop, with a voice like truck wheels on gravel. He's spent forty years in the NBA, first as a player and then as a winning head coach of four different franchises across the league. He led the Boston Celtics to an NBA title in 2008, set a franchise record for victories with the LA Clippers in 2014, and in 2020–2021 he turned the Philadelphia 76ers into a contender for the first time in twenty years.

Rivers's no-stats philosophy was formed as a player, an All-Star for the Atlanta Hawks in the late 1980s. One night, Rivers went off for thirty-seven points. With two minutes left he had the team up by twenty, and he motioned to the sideline that he wanted to come out of the game and let a younger player clean up and get some experience. But his coach Bob Weiss wanted to leave him in.

"You have a chance to get your career high," Weiss said.

Rivers thought about it for a moment, and replied, "So what?"

Rivers fervently believes a player is better off not focusing on scoring, but on the elements that lead to teamwork, such as disciplined movement without the ball and sound defense. "If I had thirty-nine, I was going to be a better person?" Rivers asked rhetorically, telling the story years later. "To me, you do your job, and wherever you stop doing it, you stop doing it for the right reasons."[2]

Smartphones threaten to get in the way of those precepts. They are chock-full of distracting and mentally distorting material. Guys pick up their phones to check their numbers, and see a message from their agents telling them what they should do, as opposed to what their team needs them to do. Rivers calls the devices the Bad News Phones. He tells his assistant coaches, "Whatever news they're getting on the phone, it's not in our favor."[3]

"No one on those phones is telling them, 'You should pass

DISCIPLINE: THE FRAMEWORK

more,'" Rivers has observed. "No one is telling them the reason they're not playing more is they don't play defense hard enough."[4]

But what is Rivers supposed to do about it? How is Rivers supposed to make players who are seven feet tall and 280 pounds do anything they don't want to do? Even if Rivers could find an effective way to enforce the rule, it would likely be self-defeating, breeding buried resentment or resistance in his players, most of whom are grown men, some of them with children, and whose strong self-will Rivers prizes.

At the end of the 2020 season, Rivers compared notes on the issue with Golden State Warriors head coach Steve Kerr, during The Ringer network's podcast series *Flying Coach*, in which bench leaders talk tradecraft. Kerr encountered the same cell phone–social media issue in his Golden State Warriors locker room. It was a daily challenge to secure the undivided concentration of young players for whom reaching for electronic devices had become a reflex.

"It's interesting because you have to decide as a coach in the modern era, am I going to be the coach that says no phones?" Kerr said. "Am I going to be that guy? Like, the old-school guy: *Hey! No phones!*"[5]

The answer to the question in the case of Rivers and Kerr was no—they weren't going to be that guy. "It's just not realistic," Kerr said. "I don't think it would work these days." Both men believed any coach who tried strong-arm attempts at enforcement would wind up with a roomful of malcontents, or doormats. Instead, they searched for ways to handle the problem with light suggestion or sarcasm. On one occasion Rivers walked into a locker room, saw a player jabbing at his phone, and cracked to him, "Tell her I said, 'Hi.'" The teasing remark made it clear the texting was an intrusion, but it left self-determination intact. A murmur of laughter ran around the room, and players put their phones down—for once.[6]

That even the most authoritative coaches in the NBA struggle over whether to forbid social media in their locker rooms says something important about discipline: it's a perplexing subject and instilling it is tremendously difficult. There may be no concept more misunderstood, misconstrued, or misapplied by poor leaders, some of whom interpret it as strictness, to be imposed on others with penalty, punishment, or spittle-flying harangue. Only to find out that they've lost the room. Disney chairman Bob Iger observes, "Using the word is very dangerous in terms of how you treat or manage people."[7]

Discipline is of course essential to good decision-making. Without it, a leader is left to sift through unreliable factors and behaviors in making choices, and the result is haphazardness, the quickest way to sabotage any endeavor. With shared discipline, uniform standards are set. Consistent attitudes and practices make results easier to analyze and the wrong calls or weak links more detectable. All actions and their causes and effects become cleaner, and clearer.

But it's just as important to understand what discipline is not. Discipline is not petty militaristic enforcement. No full-grown professional happily accepts someone else's orders unless he or she lives in a barracks.

Take the Detroit Lions in 2020. Confronted with a dictatorial head coach in Matt Patricia, the locker room rebelled, and he was fired after just two and a half years. Patricia had arrived with an excellent résumé: he spent several years as a defensive coach with the New England Patriots, where he imbibed all the elements of Bill Belichick's highly regimented "Patriot Way." The problem was, Patricia tried to impose his "way" on the Lions with methods that players found degrading rather than disciplining. Patricia banned music from the locker room on game day. He forbade the common practice of swapping jerseys with opposing players after games.[8]

"I'm on a crusade to eliminate bad football," he brayed to *The Athletic*. The statement was demeaning—the Lions didn't play bad football. They were a visibly good team that had won at least nine games in three of four previous seasons and made the play-offs twice under their well-respected former coach Jim Caldwell, who was plenty disciplined. And they had a superb quarterback and future Super Bowl winner in Matt Stafford.

Patricia's autocratic manner was accompanied by veering personal habits. He had a blisteringly foul mouth that was the furthest thing from disciplined. Players described to Bleacher Report journalist Kalyn Kahler how they would sit in meeting rooms waiting for the head coach—who was late—only for him to walk in and yell, "Okay, everybody shut the fuck up!"

On one occasion in a team-wide film meeting, Patricia put up a photograph that cornerback Darius Slay had posted of himself on social media lined up against a rival receiver. Slay had written a caption complimenting his opponent. In front of the entire room, Patricia told Slay, "Stop sucking that man's dick." Slay sat quivering with rage. He was a three-time Pro Bowl player, regarded as one of the top players in the entire league at his position, whose respect for opponents had never compromised his play—he led the league in interceptions in 2017. Slay kept his temper, but he lost all regard for Patricia and would shortly leave the team in a trade and go on to more Pro Bowl seasons with the Philadelphia Eagles.[9]

Safety Glover Quin delivered a scathing description of Patricia's effect on him to Kahler: "When you are cursing me like I am a little boy—hold on, bro, you don't have to talk to me like that to get your point across. We are partners, we are working together. . . . Don't talk to me like you own me."

According to Quin, Patricia's overbearing manner fatally compromised the Lions' trust in his decision-making: "When you are getting talked to in a disrespectful way, then every decision that happens, you start to feel like Coach don't care about us, Coach don't respect us. Going outside to practice in the cold, it is what it is. But when you felt like the Coach don't respect you, now it feels like punishment that we got to go outside in the snow, right?"[10]

The Lions finished dead last in their division in both of Patricia's full seasons. In 2020, his fragmentary third year, they went 4-7 and suffered their first shutout since 2009. Which finally provoked his firing.

Overflexing of authority is not discipline, and it fails. Patricia's example suggests that the personality assessment expert Robert Hogan is right when he observes that poor leaders are not lacking in some essential quality, but rather they tend to suffer an excess of an undesirable one, "the wrong stuff": 65 to 75 percent of employees report that their biggest problem at work is their immediate boss. Ironically, dictatorial behaviors actually amount to a *lack* of personal discipline while masquerading as a demand for it in others: a tyrannical bent, disproportionate responses to picayune issues—these things are the antithesis of a sound, disciplined decision-maker, and the people under them sense it.[11]

Hogan writes: "The most important question we ask of potential leaders is, 'Can we trust you not to abuse the privilege of authority.'"[12]

By determining what discipline is *not*, the great deciders arrive at a more nuanced definition and cultivation of it.

Discipline is not obedience.

If you want obedience, have a child.

Even with children, though, the aim of any type of discipline is to eventually make forced compliance unnecessary. The end goal is a mature being who is capable of charting his or her own direction. Steve Kerr's parents were more interested in teaching their son *self*-control than in curbing a disposition so tempestuous that he regularly embarrassed them in public. "I was a disaster as a kid with my temper because I was so competitive," he confesses.[13]

One Easter when he was about seven Kerr lost the annual egg hunt, failing to find the golden egg hidden in a garden. He dissolved into a weeping, screeching tantrum. "I completely broke down crying and throwing a fit, and everybody thought I was crazy," he says. "And I was. I couldn't help it; that's just who I was." Malcolm and Ann Kerr were college professors at UCLA, who prided themselves on their rationality, and this hyperreactive son baffled them.

But the Kerrs understood that trying to constrain him would not have worked—compression only creates more combustion. Instead, they sought to channel his temper, with some fortunate assistance from the legendary basketball coach John Wooden. UCLA was in the midst of its run of ten championships in twelve seasons under Wooden (1967–1975), and Malcolm Kerr enrolled Steve in Wooden's summer camp. It was a life-altering influence. Wooden loathed what he called emotionalism, which he viewed as a form of personal weakness. He himself had won the hard victory over his own temper as a young man. "Control your emotion or emotion will control you" was one of his sayings.[14]

On the first day of camp, Kerr learned what a stickler for self-discipline Wooden was. The coach stared down the littlest boys and told them that before they did anything else every morning, before any camp activity could begin, they were to tie their dormitory keys to their sneakers with their shoelaces. He would not tolerate lost keys, and the boys were responsible for their own. Competitive character, Wooden told the boys, started with the smallest items. "Self-control in little things leads to control of bigger things," he liked to say.[15]

It was Kerr's inaugural lesson in the discipline required of athletes. "It was like, the first thing we do in morning is to take care of any little details, and only then we could go on and play," Kerr recalls. "No detail was too small."[16]

Kerr's temperament remained a work in progress throughout his adolescence, his competitive intensity flaring obnoxiously to the continual "puzzlement" of the rest of the family. He was an overwrought, sweat-flushed striver who seethed over every loss. His parents dealt with it by displaying their own self-discipline. At Kerr's games while all the other parents yelled urgently at their kids from the stands, they would sit quietly, undemonstrative. After the game, he would simmer in the car ride on the way home, as they listened with detached calm. They'd wait patiently, until he cooled off, before saying anything.

Later, after some of the heat had gone out of him and he was capable of listening, they'd try to explain, like Wooden, that his temper only compounded his problems—when opponents saw him flustered, they knew where his weaknesses were. Kerr gradually became aware that his parents possessed composure, a source of real command in any contest. By the time Kerr reached high school, "I learned to at least pretend like I was composed," he says. "Where I'd make a mistake in a game and be furious with myself and could pretend that I wasn't bothered. It took me quite a long time for that."[17]

Today when Kerr is asked to give advice to parents of sports prodigies, he replies, "Keep your mouth shut. Just shut up."[18] What he means is that obedience is merely a grudging, forced, external result. What Kerr's parents seeded in him was not obedience, but conscience, the internal awareness that blooms into self-possession.

One definition of discipline, then, is that it's a form of self-rule.

With this definition in mind—rule of self—it becomes easier to think about the worth of all *other* kinds of rules. When you overregulate with unimportant rules, as Patricia demonstrated, you cheapen the important ones, blur distinctions between the things that really matter and those that don't. What sorts of rules, then, create the discipline that leads to high performance? For this question, let's turn from children to collegians, people grown enough to have car keys, yet who may still have issues with impulse control, and are in need of some regulation.

Query the greatest collegiate coaches about rules and what you find is that they don't like them. Former head coaches Mike Krzyzewski of Duke and Pat Summitt of Tennessee won more games than anyone in NCAA history, and they *hated* dealing with rules. Krzyzewski has observed that rulebooks turn people into petty bureaucrats, diverted from the real work of leading. Asked once by Duke sports psychology professor Greg Dale to explain his approach to organizational discipline, Krzyzewski replied, "So, the first thing is to not have too many rules."[19]

"I don't want to be a manager or a dictator," Krzyzewski reflected. "I want to be a leader—and leadership is ongoing, adjustable, flexible, and dynamic."[20]

Krzyzewski's philosophy may not satisfy people looking for a clear-cut system they can import. But good discipline, he has long maintained, is actually the function of just one rule for a whole organization: "Don't do anything that is detrimental to yourself because if you do something that is detrimental to yourself, you will be doing something that is detrimental to the team." The rule is based in the simple reality that everything you do has a bearing on someone else. If you are rude in a restaurant, then the entire group will have a reputation for being rude to waiters. If you miss an assignment, then the entire squad will be branded shirkers. If you lie, then your colleagues will be regarded as potentially un-truthful. "If you are weak in a crucial moment, then we are all going to be weak," Krzyzewski has said.

That one rule will take care most of situations before they happen, Krzyzewski believed. The sole purpose of Krzyzewski's sanctions was to convince players that "they are responsible to something bigger than themselves. . . . And you don't get that by having 20 different rules for Duke Basketball."[21]

Still, twenty-year-olds with surging adrenals and illusions of invincibility are at times inclined to make decisions detrimental to themselves and irresponsible to others. What then?

A case in point was Duke's Grayson Allen, a star guard for the Blue Devils from 2016 to 2019, who posed perhaps the most complicated disciplinary dilemma in Krzyzewski's career. Allen was a puzzling contradiction. He was in some ways a model player, excellent student, hardworking in practice, unselfish on the court, voted a team captain. He was also the kind of antago-nistic player that Duke opponents love to hate, clean-cut on the surface but with a buried edge, and in his case a provocative habit of committing hard, flagrant fouls. Early in his career at Duke, Allen intentionally tripped an unsuspecting Louisville opponent, sending him to the floor. Krzyzewski benched Allen for a few minutes and after the game made Allen apologize. Allen was "a good kid," who had done "a bad thing," Krzyzewski said in his postgame press conference. But then came another incident— and then another.

In Allen's third offense in the space of ten months, he surreptitiously leg-whipped a player from Elon after getting beat on defense. Whistled for an intentional foul and a technical, Allen went to the bench, where he came completely unstrung, screaming into his hands until he shivered. The following morning Krzyzewski suspended Allen "indefinitely." The vagueness of it did nothing to satisfy critics, who blasted Krzyzewski for not being firm. "I handle things the way I handle them," Krzyzewski declared. ". . . and I don't need to satisfy what other people think I should do. And I'm a teacher and a coach, and I'm responsible for that kid. So I know him better than anybody."[22]

The press clamored for Krzyzewski to make an example of Allen, at peril of being branded a hypocrite—someone who preached values but tolerated a cheap-shotter because he was a key player. Radio personality Dan Patrick pressed Krzyzewski on how many games Allen would sit out. But Krzyzewski refused to cave to outside opinion. "There's no Ten Commandments of tripping," he said. "God didn't send down a number of games. Each kid, each situation, is different."[23]

Allen's on-court ugliness was a situational personality, Krzyzewski believed, that didn't reflect the whole person. Allen himself seemed mystified—and frustrated—by his own behavior. "It was never this predetermined thing, 'I'm going to trip somebody,' " Allen said later.[24] Off the court, Allen was one of the most disciplined students Krzyzewksi ever had, who would make Academic All-American for four straight years, one of only four Duke players to ever do so in the coach's tenure. Allen was "not a good student, he's been a *great* student," Krzyzewski would comment at the end of Allen's collegiate career.[25]

Complicating Krzyzewski's handling of Allen was that he sympathized with a player who regularly underwent public scalding from hostile crowds. The Duke Blue Devils were habitually jeered for their seeming privilege, elitism, and perceived arrogance, and also envied for routinely hanging championship banners. Some Dukies got it worse than others, those whose haircuts were too preppy-neat and their expressions too supercilious. Some nineteen-year-olds simply weren't prepared for it. The public attention at Duke "wears on you," even Krzyzewski would confess in a last press conference shortly before he retired in 2022. Allen, perhaps more than any other player, seemed to personify the archetype: he was too smooth by half, and he seemed to wear a perennial smirk on his baby face, which opponents wanted to wipe off. Crowds taunted him with a special vitriol for every mistake and missed shot, and he lashed back. It was a function of an insecure player combatively overfiring in a pressure-cooker.[26]

Krzyzewski had to decide, what was the ultimate goal of any discipline he issued to Allen? The goal wasn't to satisfy others with a public show trial. The goal was to grow a mature performer.

Krzyzewski suspended Allen for just three games. If Allen wanted any kind of career, he had to learn to get ahold of himself and not come so unlaced. And the kid couldn't work on that while sitting on the bench or being suspended from the program. He had to confront his worst urges in the fire of competition. College players weren't yet full-grown men—they were still adolescents, in fact—but they were expected to handle the performance load like men. It was Krzyzewski's role as a collegiate coach to mediate that central tension, to help balky players like Allen to "cross bridges," as Krzyzewski put it, into adulthood.

After the benching, Allen settled down enough to secure a future as a player. In his senior season there were no major incidents, and he became a first-round NBA draft pick. Allen wasn't cured overnight—he would still show his flagrant urges in the NBA—but he would evolve into a more emotionally dependable player who even won some fans.[27]

"There are bridges people have to cross in order to fulfill their potential, [to allow for] what their talent and motivation can do for them," Krzyzewski remarked later on a podcast with his former player JJ Reddick. Discipline in this instance was about learning "the price that you have to pay to be successful, and what it took to be on a stage," Krzyzewski observed.[28]

If discipline is not enforcement, or punishment, then what is it? Discipline is the voluntary regulating of behavior that drives repetitive excellence. Successful performers develop strong personal and institutional habits that are like clockwork. Discipline therefore is not an imposed construct, but rather a fostered inner construct.

Pat Summitt talked about discipline as a kind of drivetrain. "It's the internal mechanism that self-motivates you," she said. "It gets you out of bed in the morning. It gets you to work on time and it tells you when you need to work late."[29]

And while it can be fostered, it can't be compulsory, which threatens to ruin the entire point: to create a self-perpetuating ethic.

Summitt used to tell her players, "Discipline yourselves, so no one else has to." Discipline was not "temporary behavior control," she liked to say. She was after something much more durable and long-lasting in the people she coached. Though she had a reputation as ironfisted, in fact, like Krzyzewski, she usually handled behavioral problems with finesse. When freshman Nikki McCray was late to meetings, Summitt didn't punish her. She got her a wristwatch, after learning that the kid had never owned one. "I don't treat 'em all the same," Pat liked to say. "I treat 'em all fair." McCray went on to be an Olympian and a WNBAer, and a head coach herself.[30]

Pat only had one rule that she was inflexible on: if players cut class without an excuse, they sat on the bench for the next game. She never wavered because it was less a rule than a necessity. She had no intention of wasting scholarships on undependable players who might be ineligible because they didn't make their grades. She wanted players who "self-selected," as she put it, who were not infantilized wards but whose personal rigor met her own. "Maintaining the integrity of your interior philosophy is crucial, even if it costs you a player," Summitt said. "Otherwise, your structure will collapse." She meant it. She had a high transfer rate: in thirty-eight years, a total of thirty-four players left the team for one reason or another, a rate of almost one per year. "Tennessee isn't for everybody," she would say. "If they all loved it, we'd be doing something wrong."[31]

Pat preferred *peer-adopted* discipline. She counted on a small handful of player-leaders to "take ownership" and keep teammates accountable to one another, so that issues didn't reach her office. She told them, "Your business is your business—unless I hear about it. Then it becomes my business."[32]

Perhaps the best disciplinarian-leader she ever had was Nicky Anosike, one of eight children from a Staten Island project, whose mother, Ngozi, had put herself through night school while working multiple jobs. When Pat would run the team through a three-hour practice and teammates would bend over gasping and pulling at their shorts, Anosike would tell them, "You're not tired. My *mother's* tired." The whole team would stand up straight and start sprinting again. Anosike was so disciplined that she made the dean's list every single year while carrying a triple major in political science, criminal justice, and legal studies, for which she would be named the NCAA Woman of the Year in 2008.[33]

Anosike reflected later to journalist Maria Cornelius of the Tennessee website GoVols247, "As great as Pat was, Pat wasn't going to do our job. There were some things Pat didn't have to tell us to do, i.e., work hard. There were some things she didn't have to waste her time or breath saying or doing."[34]

Anosike also remarked of her role as the team enforcer, "It starts with you giving one hundred percent. Then guess what? People respect you. Then they're more likely to listen when you have something to say."[35]

As a junior, Anosike wrote up a contract establishing players' obligations to the team and asked them to show their commitment by signing it. Every single member did. At that point, Pat knew the team could contend for the national championship—and, in fact, they went on to win back-to-back titles. One provision in the pact was that the team would forgo liquor in season, a sacrifice that Pat acknowledged on the night they won the 2007 title, when she ordered a full bar sent up to her hotel suite—and turned her back while the team carried it to their rooms.[36]

On those occasions when Summitt did step in, it was never punishment for its own sake. There was always a larger point about the identity of the program. Example: Her teams always sprinted from end to end of the floor. It was their signature; they ran so hard it made opponents wince. On one occasion when her team played lackadaisically against Notre Dame, Pat brought them from the locker room back into the arena after the game was over. "We're going to run a little bit more, because we didn't do it in the game," she told them. She figured they had only played hard for thirty minutes of the forty-minute game, she said, so before they could get on the bus to go home they had to put in ten more minutes of running the floor. She didn't run them ragged; she merely made a point: this is what we do.[37]

Watching from the eaves was Notre Dame's young coach Muffet McGraw. "She brought her team out to run extra—in *my* arena," McGraw said. "I was like, *Wow*. It was one of those things where you look at it and go, 'Hmmmm, maybe there is something to that.'"[38]

The episode left a lasting impression on McGraw, who drew from it a fundamental conclusion that would influence her own coaching: The implied intent of any rule is establishing, "This is important." And if something really is *important*, then it should be important enough to emphasize every single time.

Notre Dame would become known as one of the most disciplined teams in the country under McGraw. The pace and precision in their player movement was impeccable. That was because McGraw would mark the floor with a taped X and say, "I want you here. I don't want you three inches to the right or the left. I want you *here*."

When they ran to their spaces raggedly, McGraw would halt practice. "You're going to *touch* the line," she said. "You're not going to just be in the *area*."

But it was one thing to mark the floor and it was another thing for McGraw to have the willpower to insist on that precision at the end of a three-hour practice, when she herself was tired and all she longed to do was blow the whistle so she could go home. "The biggest issue with coaching is, do you want to do it until you get it right?" McGraw told me. "Or do you get to a point of diminishing returns where you go, 'You know, it's not going to happen today, so let's move on'? Do you lower your goals? Instead of five in a row, do you try to get three in a row? And I think I was just like, '*No*, we stay till we get it right.' Because what are you teaching them, on the other end of this? If you say, 'This is the goal,' and then you don't reach it and you move on, what are you teaching them about *your* discipline?"[39]

McGraw kept the team on the floor, even when it meant an additional hour before she could go home. "I didn't settle," she says. The result: ten Final Fours and two national titles between the years 1997 and 2020.

Along the way, McGraw learned an interesting technique for putting responsibility for discipline on the players. She gave them a choice. She'd show them the practice plan, and tell them, "I think we can get this done in an hour and a half." But if they didn't get it done *right*, she said, it would probably take two and a half or three hours.

"So it's up to you," she said. "Get it right the first time."

The flip side of the clarity bred by a disciplined leader is the distrust engendered by an inconsistent one. Leaders had better be an example of personal discipline themselves if they want their decisions to work.

Seattle Seahawks coach Pete Carroll has observed, "Inconsistency is one of the greatest pitfalls" in leaderly decision-making. Oftentimes a coach, especially a young one, will set a rule in the attempt to establish authority, without having the energy or willingness to truly live out the implications of it. Players and colleagues then see a telltale lack of conviction. "Any time you deal with a situation, you're making a statement about who and what you are," Carroll has observed to The Ringer network. "And players are watching to see, do you believe in something, or are you just dealing with it randomly?"[40]

There is a special hostility reserved for leaders who treat standards as applicable to everyone but themselves. Others experience it as a kind of duplicity; it makes them feel confused, tricked, or even taken for fools. It turns the entire organization into a charade.

A perfect example of how *not* to foster discipline in an institution was modeled by Notre Dame president John I. Jenkins in the fall of 2020. Jenkins, a thoughtful and widely admired sixty-six-year-old priest with degrees in philosophy and theology, worked hard to bring students back to campus mid-pandemic. The school issued strict protocols. Masking was mandatory and students were barred from gathering in any common rooms.

Then in September, Notre Dame law professor Amy Coney Barrett was nominated to the Supreme Court. An exultant Jenkins traveled to Washington, D.C., for a White House ceremony honoring her. At the event, Jenkins broke every rule that his students were ordered to follow. He was photographed mingling inside the White House—unmasked. He shook hands and even shared hugs with others in the Rose Garden ceremony, violating the social-distance standards and protocols he had insisted others meet.

The Rose Garden reception became a super-spreader event. After Jenkins returned to campus, he tested positive for COVID-19. The reaction was swift, sneering, and vehement. The student newspaper called his conduct "embarrassing," and a petition circulated demanding his resignation. Someone even reported him to a coronavirus hotline for violating protocols.[41]

Jenkins quickly issued an apology. "I failed to lead by example," he acknowledged. But events conspired to expose him to maximum condemnation. The campus experienced a broad virus outbreak—at one point by mid-fall there would be almost fourteen hundred cases on campus, with a test positivity rate of 5 percent. Students broke rules at a large party and flooded the football field in throngs after a big victory, and wondered aloud why they should comply with protocols their school president had flouted. How much weight could Jenkins's edicts have, given that he had showed no more command of himself in the White House Rose Garden than a whooping, field-rampaging fan? Notre Dame would struggle throughout the fall and winter to contain the virus.[42]

The ire at Jenkins eventually abated, but his authority took an undeniable hit. "The Moral Failure of Father John Jenkins," read a headline in the prestigious *Chronicle of Higher Education*.[43]

The best deciders understand that they'd better live the expectations they set for others. "Not tolerating a breakdown in integrity is about walking the talk as much as talking it," says Disney's Iger.[44]

Smaller matters of disciplined conduct, such as how to speak to people at work, pile up over time into credence. Hogan has observed that when a leader makes sound, disciplined decisions all day long, day after day, "the quality of their decisions accumulates" and they gain in the estimation of those who follow them. Almost like a batting average.[45]

No one in sports lived out the concept of daily personal discipline more than Derek Jeter, or won more trust with it, chosen as captain of the New York Yankees eleven times. In sports, scores and statistics tell the story of someone's decisions over the long haul. Jeter's hitting stats, his lifetime batting average of .310, was a reflection of his small daily discipline for twenty years. Over those two decades, Jeter went to bed at the same time every night during the season.

Baseball games end at around 11:00 p.m. No matter what town he was in, who he was with, or what tempted him, Jeter was in bed and asleep two hours later. His teammates, friends, and romantic partners understood that he was simply "unavailable" socially between April when the season began and November when it ended. Jeter's rewards and records reflected this consistency, with five World Series titles, fourteen All-Star appearances, and the Yankees' all-time marks for hits, and times on base.[46]

Jeter's unvarying routine gave former Yankees director of performance Dana Cavalea a simple crossover insight. Cavalea, who now advises CEOs and executives on how to train for high performance, says, "Set habits lead to more predictable and favorable outcomes." It's that simple.[47]

Whenever he saw a player with scattered habits, who did one thing on Monday, another on Tuesday, and still another on Wednesday, Cavalea knew he was looking at someone who would wind up back in the minor leagues. He sees the same in business managers. "What I find to be the difference between athletes and executives is, that athletes are very disciplined in the right things and a lot of executives are disciplined in the wrong things," Cavalea says. Type A hard chargers often misapprehend what constitutes personal discipline and confuse it with overwork. "They're masters at burying themselves," Cavalea says. "They're constantly putting themselves in a position of deficit."[48]

One of their worst habits is to let urgencies of the day overtake their agenda. They're so reactive and in crisis mode that they decide they don't have time to work out. Which is why Cavalea's first step with a new client is to help him or her revise their schedule, with boundaries for when it begins and ends. Personal discipline begins by taking charge of your daily calendar, so that decisions are not imposed on you. "If you're saying this is how *I* do things, you'll be amazed at how things and people start to adapt to you, as opposed to you feeling like you have to constantly adapt to them and to these problems and circumstances," Cavalea says. Daily discipline has an enormous side benefit: a sense of controlling the controllables.[49]

A common mistake most of us make in trying to be more disciplined is to adopt a whole slew of new habits all at once. And then we quit or revert after a day or two when it's hard. Cavalea advises: start with one small change—say, an absolute commitment to work out—and master it a minute, hour, and day at a time. Athletes teach that you can only win the big things by winning the moment with good micro-decisions.

They keep themselves on the grind by asking themselves the question: Can you stay disciplined, even if it's uncomfortable, for just a minute longer? Most of us judge the worth of an activity by how it feels in the moment. But athletes judge the worth of an action *by how they feel when they are done*. This is a fundamental outlook anyone can borrow from, and you don't have to be Derek Jeter to practice it. The physical strain of training doesn't feel good for anyone who is gasping for breath, but afterwards there is a sense of command from having done something difficult. With negative behaviors—especially ones involving sugar—it's exactly reversed. It feels awfully good at the time, only to be followed by the re-re's: regret and self-recrimination.

Personal discipline is admittedly monotonous, and some people interpret it as deadening. "It makes them feel sort of expired," Cavalea observes. But the secret of successful deciders is that they train themselves into a higher tolerance for tedium, and in time their better habits begin to feel gratifying rather than denying. "Discipline is a muscle, too," Cavalea says. "The more we do it, the more it allows us to become more confident in what it is that we're doing, and more importantly, in who we are."[50]

Discipline means rejecting average habits, refusing to cut a corner, resisting the pressure of the crowd, not drinking at a social dinner, not partaking in the group dessert, refusing to relax your routine, in danger of being called a stiff. "When you're disciplined, with it also comes friction," Cavalea says. "Because you're not just doing what everyone else is doing. You're going to have to start making choices." But with those choices comes the knowledge that you're doing something that others aren't willing to, and which will set you apart.

Believe this: disciplined people are not *average*. They are determined to be above average. And maybe even alone at the top.

"Unsuccessful people are consistent too," Cavalea points out. "Don't ever forget that."[51]

The ultimate misconstruction of discipline is that it is somehow inhibiting, the opposite of choice. In fact, discipline is liberating. The late Harvey A. Dorfman, a renowned mental performance coach for Major League Baseball pitchers, put it better than anyone. "Self-discipline is a form of freedom," he remarked. "Freedom from laziness and lethargy, freedom from the expectations and demands of others, freedom from weakness and fear and doubt."[52]

The person who is more disciplined is the person who creates options for him- or herself—career options, style of living options, financial options—and thus has the best chance of making the "right" call.

5.

Candor

The Language

The right call can swing a game sometimes, but the right word at the right time, to reach someone who is drowning in insecurity—to restore, rescue even—that's infinitely more powerful. Mark Twain said the difference between the right word and the almost-right word is "the difference between the lightning bug and the lightning." Coaches therefore will tell you that the "pep talk" is largely a myth: high performers are almost impossible to manipulate with counterfeit speeches, they say. What turns a performance is the truth.[1]

The truth is what got Diana Nyad through her record swim from Cuba to Florida in 2013. There was no room on such a trip for anything else—a false word would have been the quickest route to danger. Which was why Nyad and her coach and team director, Bonnie Stoll, had a hard rule for the crew that shepherded Nyad on the 110-mile odyssey through the Florida Strait.

"No sarcasm," ordered Stoll.[2]

All endeavors essentially begin in dark waters. According to the distinguished management-studies scholar Henry Mintzberg, a principal dilemma for every leader is how to recognize the need for action amid a cloud of vague, murky reports. The vital first step for a good leader, then, is to spell things out, to "clarify and define the issues." He or she has to identify the problem and the purpose and meaning of an action, and why it's important, in language as clear and illuminating as a lightning strike.[3]

Nyad's Cuba expedition made Mintzberg's decisional dark waters seem like a mere tub bath. It was first and foremost a communications challenge. The swim would be an out-of-category piece of cartography, the equivalent of five English Channels, that would require Nyad to thrash for almost sixty continuous hours through an ocean subject to unpredictable currents and sudden storm bursts, with her head submerged, visible at night only by a small red light on her cap. Following her was a flotilla of shark divers, escort kayaks, oceanographers, meteorologists, and a pulmonologist, all on different boats, trying to watch her for signs of distress in the murk. Nyad simply couldn't afford a facetious tenor.

"If people start talking shit or talking sarcastically, they're not doing their job," Stoll says. "If you're saying, 'Hey, so and so said . . . ,' then you aren't concentrating."[4]

A wrong or cross word could lead to confusion and tensions on the crew under pressure. Nyad was utterly reliant on a clear series of relayed decisions about continually shifting factors from wave heights to wildlife. If there was a break in the chain, then there would be, potentially, a gap in the surveillance. Nyad couldn't afford gaps, not when she was swimming through liquid acreage populated by whitetip sharks and lethal jellyfish. It was a monotonous but tense undertaking that required around-the-clock teamwork, without any chance of misinterpretation or feuding.

"There are egos and insecurities that act themselves out within any group working together," Nyad observes. "And in this case, there was history to be made, there was media, and those elements could have easily led to infighting over territory. Each person had a very specific job, in some cases, jobs that could wind up life-or-death situations. Bonnie was insistent that our crew would be entirely free of gossip, of backbiting."[5]

Stoll was a sun-burnished, powerfully energetic woman with an assertive voice and her own natural buoyancy. She was a close friend of Nyad's and almost as fit, a former pro racquetballer who rose to No. 3 in the world before becoming a renowned physical trainer in Los Angeles with a list of celebrity clients. She was perceptive and unintimidated in dealing with high achievers. Stoll could issue directives to Nyad and the crew in a tone of firm yet cheerful competence, which the *New Yorker* magazine described as "that of an exceptionally jovial drill sergeant."[6]

"She's clear and she's strong and there's not a lot of smooth talking around it," Nyad said of her. "And it works for me."[7]

Their Cuba odyssey had begun with Nyad's turning sixty. It rankled her that great athletic feats were only supposed to be for ephemeral youths. As a young woman in her twenties Nyad had been the greatest open water endurance swimmer in the world, who won fame with treacherous trips like a circuit around the island of Manhattan. But she had failed at her most ambitious attempt, a swim from Havana to Key West in 1978. It had ended after forty-nine hours and forty-one minutes in seven-foot peaks and was the only large body of water she couldn't conquer.[8] Nyad retired and didn't swim a lap for the next thirty years, parlaying

an ebullient personality and incisive intelligence into a long career as a TV commentator. But her sixtieth birthday awakened
a long-dormant sense of competitive discontent; she missed "the
high of commitment." Nyad began to do laps again at a club pool,
with a view to trying the Cuba epic again. When the workouts
grew to four hours at a stretch, she confessed what she had in
mind to Stoll, who was intrigued by the idea of a sixty-year-old
woman expanding the notions of physical capability.

They began to plot the logistics of a potential Cuba journey,
using a whiteboard and Magic Marker. But first they had to raise
the money—it would take at least $350,000 in boats and crew to
support the expedition. Nyad had to make a persuasive pitch to
sponsors, and somehow convince them that it was doable.

"I am not getting out unless I'm eaten by a shark or unconscious," she declared.[9] During one cocktail party to raise funds
for the venture Nyad enlivened the crowd by rolling up a sleeve
and popping a bicep muscle the size of a small cannonball. Conversation stopped, replaced by sharp intakes of breath. Nyad announced, in a voice full of certainty, "I feel I'm in a prime."

The checkbooks came out. It was the first communications
triumph of the trip.

The larger communications challenge was organizational. In
the beginning, Stoll was one of a half-dozen co-equal "handlers"
appointed by Nyad to manage the crossing project. But as the
training intensified and crew grew to thirty-five members—all
volunteers—it became apparent that Nyad needed a single exchange point. The others began to defer to Stoll. It was never
explicitly declared, but it became apparent that Stoll was the
most authoritative person on the boats.

Stoll enjoyed training challenges, and for months she had
quietly done the most homework of anyone in the crew. She re-

searched nutrition and devised ginger pastes that Nyad could keep down when she was nauseated to the point of retching from swallowing salt water. She learned that high-acid fruits would counteract how the salt made Nyad's mouth swell. Of all the handlers, Stoll was the person who gave the most of her own time—she never missed a single training swim.

Stoll studied Nyad closely. She knew there would be times when nonverbal communication was crucial and she had to be able to identify when Nyad might have a problem she couldn't articulate. One afternoon, as Nyad swam laps in a Los Angeles pool for twelve straight hours Stoll brought a beach chair and a cooler, parked herself right next to Nyad's lane, and followed Nyad's pace with a stopwatch for the entire day. She took notes on her pace and the chop of her arms. Sometimes she'd ask Nyad what song she was playing her head, so she understood her rhythm. Stoll learned that Nyad's sweet spot was between 52 and 55 strokes per minute. If she went faster, she'd tire too easily, and if she slowed, it meant something was wrong; she was hurt, tired, or sick.

During an open-water training session in Key West, the weather turned so stormy that Nyad canceled the boats and gave the crew the day off. She intended to train alone in the rain at a lagoon used by the Coast Guard for diving drills. Stoll insisted on going along. She sat on an open dock, in a deluge, for eight hours as Nyad did laps. Occasionally Nyad would pop up and tell Stoll to go find an overhang or sit in the car. Stoll wouldn't do it. Partly, Stoll stayed so she could observe how Nyad dealt with the swells and sheets of wind-driven rain. But she also did it to build communicative trust. "She weathered through that heavy downpour all day long, not wanting me to think she would take it easy when I was working so hard," Nyad observed.[10]

Stoll's constant presence allowed her to gauge the depth of Nyad's physical and mental stamina. On a twenty-four-hour training swim around Saint Martin, Nyad was buffeted by strong winds late in the night. By the eighteen-hour mark she was in such a state of exhaustion that she was nearly incoherent. Stoll called her close to the boat for a talk. "Do you have five strokes left in you?" Stoll asked. Nyad replied in a weary voice, "I think so."

"Let me see those five strokes, Diana," said Stoll. "There's no shame in eighteen hours, especially in these fierce winds. If you can't do five, then we'll pack it up. But put your head down and show me if you can do those five strokes."

Nyad took five tentative strokes. When she raised her head from the water, Stoll was holding five fingers up. Five more. Nyad plunged ahead for five more paces. She looked up, and there was the palm again. Five more. Stoll coaxed her slowly, five by five, until Nyad had recovered her trawling rhythm. A crease of light appeared on the horizon. Stoll suspected that with the first light of dawn Nyad would get a second wind. And she did. "My hopes revived, and my body revived," Nyad says. Nyad completed the swim—and her faith in Stoll's judgment was cemented by the exchange.

On August 7, 2011, after nearly two years of training and prep, Nyad jumped off a rock on the Cuban shore into the gulf and launched her official attempt to cross to Key West. She was wearing only a singlet, a pair of goggles, and some grease. Under the rules of open water swimming, she would not be able to so much as hold on to the side of a boat if the swim was to be a legitimate record. Stoll perched on the starboard side of the lead craft. For the duration of the trip, Stoll never left her post, except to go to the bathroom. At night, she wore a headlamp so that Nyad could see that she was still there.

The pyramid of communications in the flotilla—all of the operational discussions among crew over ship radio channels and walkie-talkies—ultimately narrowed to that figure on the prow. Stoll was the tactical commander who filtered through input from navigators and meteorologists to make tough calls. When John Bartlett, the lead navigator, wanted to know if Nyad could swim at a faster pace in order to beat a tough current, it was Stoll he went to. She was the one who could read Nyad's body language and pace in the water, see distress in her, and determine if she was capable of a higher cadence.

For communication to be clear, it had to be well channeled. They developed a second rule: nobody talked to Nyad but Stoll. As Nyad rose and fell through the troughs and swells, she was sensory deprived, in a state of absolute physical desolation, and confused. After a sleepless day and night of steady stroking through salt water, it was not uncommon for her to become disoriented, and even hallucinatory. Once, she thought she saw the Seven Dwarfs in the water. Nyad needed a single recognizable voice who could penetrate her exhaustion and confusion in the water. That voice was Stoll's.

Stoll and Nyad had a third imperative rule of communication on the trip, which came just after "no sarcasm" and clear channeling: no one was to *ever* tell Nyad how long she had been swimming or how far she had to go.

Guesses and chatter about time and distance were useless, given the shifting tides and currents. It was 110 miles from Havana to Key West. If a crew member looked at a GPS and saw they were fifty-five miles off Havana, and said, "Hey, you're halfway there!" it would almost inevitably be wrong and set Nyad up for a mental crash. Myriad things could happen—"and usually did," Nyad reflected wryly. A tropical storm could sweep her south, or a warm swirling eddy could push her counterclockwise, and add miles to the journey. In 1978, winds had pushed her so far off course she was headed for Brownsville, Texas, before she surrendered.

Stoll and Nyad viewed the swim like a space mission: NASA didn't celebrate when the rocket was *close* to landing on Mars. Anything could happen on the descent. The rule was, nobody was to tell Nyad where she was until she was standing upright and walking on sand.

"Bonnie was adamant in enforcing the 'don't tell her what time it is, don't tell her how far we've come or how far we have to go' rule," Nyad recalled. "She and I knew exactly what we needed to do and how to go about it. The perspective of how far we had traveled at any point led to inaccuracy and then discouragement, if factors happened to make us farther away than we had thought."[11]

Toward the end of the first day, one of those unpredictable factors occurred. Nyad felt a strain in her right shoulder. She treaded water while Stoll sprinkled some paracetamol into her mouth, and then continued on. But shortly afterwards, Nyad was struck by an asthma attack, possibly in reaction to the painkiller. Gasping in the growing dark, she couldn't breathe properly.

"What can I do for you, Diana?" Stoll called. "Come close to the boat and talk to me slowly, so you don't waste any breath."[12]

A medic jumped in the water and administered an inhaler to Nyad. She managed to continue for another five hours. But she was so weakened by the asthma that she couldn't mount a significant pace. She had to constantly stop and roll over on her back to breathe, and the current nullified any progress she made. Their navigator advised Stoll that they were just drifting. Nyad began to swallow seawater, which made her retch. Her body temperature dropped until she shuddered almost uncontrollably. After a total of twenty-nine hours in the water, she told Stoll she couldn't go on.

"I just can't," she said brokenly to Stoll. "Do you agree? Do you agree?"

"Are you kidding?" Stoll said sympathetically, agreeing.[13]

Once Nyad was out of the water and swathed in towels, she was frustrated. She was in the best shape of her life, and to have a freak injury stop her after just one day was intolerable. She was determined to try again.

Six weeks later, she persuaded the crew to hastily reassemble for a second attempt. This time, her shoulder felt great. Conditions were dead calm, balmy, and Nyad bounded through the glassy waters on a promising pace. As night fell, a sense of optimism pervaded the crew.

Then Nyad started screaming.

She had plowed into a swarm of box jellyfish, gelatinous creatures whose three-foot tentacles were like miniature harpoons, and potentially lethal. They injected venom so neurotoxic it could cause cardiac arrest—every year, they killed more people than sharks. Nyad felt an initial sensation like a whiplash, followed by a full-body acid wash. She writhed in the water and compulsively screamed, *"Fire! Fire! Fire! Fire!"* over and over, her eyes bulging with terror. A six-foot-two shark diver jumped in to help clear the jellyfish away and he, too, was almost overcome and required medical attention.[14]

After medic-administered doses of prednisone and some oxygen, Nyad assured Stoll she was recovered enough to keep swimming. But then she was stung again—this time in the face and neck. Incredibly, after more oxygen and rest, Nyad insisted on resuming. She intended to at least finish a "staged" swim. She had broken her continuity to board the boat for assistance, so it couldn't be considered an endurance record, but she was determined to complete the journey. She was so weak, however, that she couldn't mount a strong enough pace. Though she tried for several more hours, she was inevitably pulled eastward toward the Bahamas and wouldn't make it, the navigator told Stoll.

Stoll choked back tears and blew the whistle calling Nyad over to the boat. She gave her the truth: "You're not capable, right now, of swimming like you swim.

"There's nobody in the world who could possibly do it except you," Stoll continued. "But I watched you almost die last night. I really did. And I don't think I could do that again."

When Nyad climbed out of the water, the wounds from the jelly stings were lividly apparent. Thick red welts ran across her neck, face, back, and sides. As Nyad lay immobilized and shivering in towels, Stoll said, "Diana, look at me." Eyes wide open, Nyad made eye contact. "Listen, we'll come back and do it again."

"Promise," Nyad croaked.

"Yes."[15]

They came back a year later in August of 2012. This time, Nyad had a protective suit to don at night to shield her from the box jellyfish, which tended to appear after sunset. She swam strongly for almost two days—and then a squall struck. The shark guardians in their kayaks dove steeply into troughs, and forks of lightning flashed around them. Stoll blew the whistle and told Nyad to come out of the water.

Nyad was beside herself—she had swum for more than two straight days and nights, and still felt strong. But Stoll insisted they could not risk the safety of the crew. It was over. Nyad reluctantly acquiesced and climbed onto the boat. "I'm sort of her conscience, on some level, when she's ready to hear it," Stoll said later. If Stoll said it was over, then it was.[16]

This time, Stoll assumed it was over once and for all. There were simply too many harsh, changeable elements that defied logistical planning. But Nyad called her just a few weeks later: she had begun to think about a *fourth* attempt. Stoll was incredulous. She flatly refused to participate and told Nyad she had become unreasonably obsessed. "I didn't want her to look like the crazy cat lady," Stoll said later.[17]

Nyad waged a persuasion campaign, but Stoll was unmoving. They were at such an impasse that Stoll finally said, "Let's go talk to a mediator." She suggested the founder and CEO of the World Open Water Swimming Association, Steve Munatones, a mutual friend who had observed their previous attempts as an official record keeper. Nyad said brightly, "Oh good, he'll talk you into doing it."

"That's *not* what a mediator does," Stoll said. "He listens to both sides."

It was more than an hour's drive in heavy traffic to Munatones's home in Huntington Beach, but Stoll made it with Nyad, hoping that he might be able to reason with her. Once they arrived, Munatones listened to each of them for another hour, without saying much. Finally, Stoll asked him forthrightly, "Steve, is this swim possible?" Munatones thought for a long minute. Then he said, "It's highly improbable. But if anyone can do it, you can."[18]

They had one great asset going for them, Munatones observed: their powerful communication. Stoll knew everything to say, and not say, to Nyad in the water. She knew that Nyad's left shoulder was much stronger than her right, so if she didn't give her periodic directional guidance she would swim practically in a circle. She knew that during the sleepless nights of swimming Nyad might have hallucinations, but that they weren't dangerous, so when Nyad saw the Taj Mahal looming out of the water Stoll would just tell her to swim around it. Above all, she knew that she was dealing with someone willing to endure almost anything to succeed—who was in "a lot of pain, a *lot* of pain," Stoll says. Nyad didn't need tough love or some faux motivational speech "to get out there and swim." She needed to be paced and reassured, and no one knew how to do that for Nyad better than Stoll. "There was no yelling, no demeaning, no asking of me more than I have at any point," Nyad remarked later. "Bonnie knew that I was going to be giving too much, never the case of not enough."[19]

Stoll and Nyad's interchanges reminded Munatones of a phrase he had picked up while living in Japan for a time: *Ishin Denshin*. It meant a form of exchange so genuine and strong that it results in an unspoken mutual understanding. Stoll and Nyad had developed *Ishin Denshin*, he said. What's more, they had instilled it in the people around them. He had never seen a crew so unified, skilled, and intent on their work.

During the drive back to their homes in Los Angeles, neither Stoll nor Nyad said a word for a long time. Toward the end of the trip, Stoll broke the silence. "What if you don't make it this time?" she asked.

Nyad just glanced at her and said, "So?"

Stoll spent two days thinking over that reaction. It persuaded her that Nyad had the swim in perspective and could accept failure if she didn't make it again. She called Nyad. "You're clearly not changing your dream," she said. "If you go without me and you don't make it, it's going to be my fault. And if you go without me and you *do* make it, can you imagine how I'd feel? So I'm in."[20]

To seal the deal, they went to a tattoo parlor and got matching ink: *Ishin Denshin*.[21]

As they embarked from Cuba on their fourth try in August of 2013, for once the currents were entirely with them. When Stoll blew the whistle to bring Nyad to the boat side for a drink of electrolytes or a slab of bread and peanut butter, the eddies pushed her *toward* Key West instead of away. And when a storm blew in, the wind was from the helping direction.[22]

By the end of the second full day in the water, as dusk approached, conditions were so good that it seemed certain Nyad would finally make it. The seas still favored her, and there were no clouds on the weather map.

But it was time for the worst part of the swim. Evening calm was when the box jellyfish would emerge. Nyad swam to the boat and began to don the protective full-body suit and face mask. The suit was ingenious—and potentially lifesaving. Stoll had enlisted a world-renowned biochemist who studied venoms at the University of Hawaii, Dr. Angel Yanagihara, to work with the wet-suit company FINIS in devising it. The synthetic full-body covering included gloves, booties, and even a prosthetic mouth guard to keep the tentacles off of Nyad's tongue. But no amount of technology could make it comfortable. The suit abraded Nyad's skin and the mask cut her mouth and made her swallow seawater. She hated it.

Nyad had no idea where she was in the journey. She only knew that climbing into the suit was yet another physical torment. Unspeakably weary, her mouth so swollen by salt that she was disfigured, she struggled to pull it on.

Stoll made an executive decision. She was about to break a cardinal rule of the expedition. She was going to tell Nyad where she was.

"Diana, this is the last time you are ever going to have to put on this suit," she said.

Nyad just looked at her and said, brokenly, "We're not gonna make it?"

No, Stoll replied, that wasn't what she meant.

"I mean you're never going to have to swim at night again,"

Stoll said. "We're going to finish this swim tomorrow while it's still light out."

Nyad only had fifteen hours to go to reach the shore, Stoll told her, and there was nothing ahead but still waters.

That's just a training swim, Nyad thought to herself. *I do that all the time. I can do this.*[23]

It was the right word, at the right time. Resurgent, Nyad swam strongly through the rest of the night. At dawn, Stoll pointed to the horizon and said, "Those are the lights of Key West." Nyad wept.

She staggered onto the beach at about 2:00 p.m. on September 2, 2013, after nearly 53 continuous hours in the ocean. Nyad had finally finished the journey—at sixty-four years old, and on her fifth overall attempt. She waded through an enormous crowd that surrounded her in the surf, and sagged into Stoll's waiting arms.

Stoll's clarity, her steady presence and ready answers, had been as important to Nyad as her own limbs in making the journey successful. *Ishin Denshin*, as Nyad defined the term, was a state "whereby two people have spent such quality and quantity of time in training as to understand just what the other means, what each of them needs." They had achieved it.[24]

"To turn my head to the left for fifty-two hours and fifty-four minutes, and every single stroke, even with a dazed mind, debilitated vision, to see Bonnie's silhouette, her headlamp in the black of night, was such a profound, heartening vision for me," Nyad said later. "She was always there."[25]

Despite the bewildering assortment of problems and challenges, "we were able to work through emergencies with such clear and intelligent resolve," Nyad reflected. Nyad and Stoll's experience, for all of the failed crossings, was a supreme example of how candor in a communicative partnership could cut like a light through dark waters.

Merely giving an order is not decisional leadership; you have to persuade others to enact it with conviction. "Leaders affect organizational outcomes through other people," wrote Robert B. Kaiser, Robert Hogan, and S. Bartholomew Craig in a study of corporate dynamics, "Leadership and the Fate of Organizations." How a decision is conveyed is therefore as important as what the decision is, and profoundly impacts the chances of its success.[26]

Poor workplaces are full of vague statements delivered in a murmuring or couched way, or, worse, corporate euphemisms. Soft language may seem safe and convenient because it's slippery, inoffensive seeming. But it actually has a hard superficiality that leaves people feeling insulted. It sounds equivocating, evasive, even devious. And it breeds the opposite of belief.

Take a quarterback who makes the wrong decision and throws an interception. It's an excruciating public failure. How candidly a field leader deals with his teammates in that situation can make or break their trust in him. Former San Francisco 49ers quarterback Steve Young, now president and co-founder of a private equity firm, gives vivid descriptions of how he learned this to business audiences.

In 1991, Young was a disgruntled reserve quarterback for the San Francisco 49ers, trying to emerge from behind the great veteran Joe Montana, a four-time Super Bowl champion. Young was enormously talented, with dodging feet and an arm powerful as an air gun, but he was insecure playing in the shadow of Montana, and it showed. When Montana was lost to an elbow injury, Young finally had his chance, but he struggled to assume the communicative accountability that came with the position. Every time Young threw an interception, put the ball in an opponent's hands, he felt scrutiny, unfair comparisons because he wasn't Joe. He would jog to the sideline and try to deflect blame. "There is a moment when the team looks back at me because I just lost the game," Young told the seed company Costanoa Ventures. When players glanced at him questioningly, Young would say a receiver had "cut late." Or he'd tell them a blocker hadn't carried out the right scheme. "It inspired no one," he confessed.[27]

In a moment of key answerability to colleagues, Young parsed and excused. They lacked belief in him and finished 10-6, an unsuccessful year by their Super Bowl standards. "If you go with the mitigation route, it is disastrous," Young advised. He expanded on why "mitigation" is so harmful to a leader's effectiveness in an interview with the *San Francisco Business Times*. "On the football field I learned there are no liars," he remarked. "You've got the lines on the field, the clock, 80,000 witnesses, the score. . . . You can't hide, deflect—you're exposed, you have to live out the truth." When he started to list the mitigating factors to his teammates, "That allows everyone *else* to do mitigation—'I'm not responsible.'"

Young concluded, "If you're going to hold 10 others on the field to do things super hard in pressure, you need them in a mindset of accountability, not mitigation. . . . The only way to success is to say, 'I screwed up and I will fix it. Now I want you to come with me.'"[28]

The following season, Young went on a personal accountability campaign to regain the trust of his teammates. When he threw interceptions, instead of reacting with shoulder-curling evasion, he made himself take the blame—whether it was his fault or not—and move on. "When the crowd is booing you, when the lights are on and your teammates are asking you why," Young recalled, "you actually say, 'I screwed it up. My fault. The ball was in my hands. . . . But I'll tell you what, let's get some water and let's turn around and win the game.'"[29]

The most amazing thing happened. By communicating personal accountability in front of the entire group, "it let the other guys do the same," he remembers. On the sideline, this is what he heard:

"I cut late."

"I missed the block."

When Young began to view those moments on the field not as personal interrogations but as opportunities for trustful exchanges with his teammates, they became fascinating to him. "The best thing about playing was it helped me get this idea that there are key moments in any relationship where accountability needs to be there," he observes. "One of the best things I learned in my football career was to watch for those moments, not in the locker room, or tomorrow in film, but in the moment right there, in front of everybody."[30]

In 1992, Steve Young was the Most Valuable Player in the entire NFL, and he went on to win three Super Bowls. "Something that was miserable was actually an opportunity that spun into something well beyond anything I could have ever imagined," he concluded. ". . . In many ways I learned from the rigor around that dynamic."[31]

The phrase "locker-room talk" is associated with crudity, and there's no question that exists. But as Young illustrated, the conversation within a championship organization is also sensitive and its inhabitants are highly attuned to nuance and tone. Which is why the great leaders, no matter how loud or soft-spoken they may be, pay attention to a fine but profound distinction: the difference between blame and critique.

Blame is accusation. Critique is explanation.

If you want to breed trust, *you don't just tell someone what they did wrong; you tell them how to do it right*. Great leaders never present a problem to the team or a player without also presenting that it can be solved. They stress the remedy or resolution.

"This is very important," Hall of Fame former NFL coach Tony Dungy says. "It's easy to criticize, it's easy to be critical, but most people learn better if you say, 'This is what I'm looking for to help us. When you do *this*, we're playing great.' As opposed to, 'When you don't do this, it's terrible, and we're gonna lose.'"[32]

Dungy's observation is ratified by the studies of management scientist Paul C. Nutt, who devoted an entire career to analyzing why organizations fail. "Finding problems prompts blame . . . which prompts defensive action," Nutt explains. It's crucial for a leader to address problems in a way that drives free, honest discourse, as opposed to finger-pointing, which is not only demoralizing but creates exchanges that are the opposite of candid. "Energy is directed away from finding answers and funneled toward protecting the subordinate's back," Nutt writes politely. In other words, blame is a recipe for ass covering—and therefore more failure in the future.

It's axiomatic among the best coaches that player evaluation is most effective when you separate the performance from the person. Hard data, film, statistical analysis, and other impersonal tools can translate the conversation from blame to critique. "You are your numbers," Hall of Fame NFL coach Bill Parcells liked to say to his players. With cool, neutral sources in hand, everyone feels less attacked and becomes more involved and engaged in solution finding. "It replaces individual praise and blame with communal interest," Nutt observes. And a communal interest tends to lead to greater commitment to the next plan of action.[33]

The truth can be expressed in any number of different styles, from a sonnet to a signal to a shout. But regardless, whether it's a play call in front of seventy-five thousand or a private meeting in an office, a leader's word always has a primary aim, especially under stress: to engender alliance.

As Mike Krzyzewski once observed, strategic plans are only as good as the relationships between those who execute it. "We aren't coaching x's and o's, we are coaching people. . . . I always tell coaches that you put up these x's on the board, and if x1 hates x2 and if x3 doesn't know how to communicate with x4, then your defense is going to stink."[34]

A trove of business scholarship has been devoted to "LMX Theory," shorthand for "leader-member exchange." This is a scientific-sounding term for what otherwise might be called collegiality. Leaders who are expressive, who seek the input, understanding, and agreement of others in frank and welcoming exchanges, tend to see better results across the board.

This type of exchange doesn't just make you more persuasive or popular. It makes you a better problem solver. It leads to a better "discovery process," which in the estimate of Nutt is where so many leaders could learn to become better decision-makers. A boss who "imposes" decisions, and who blocks out others because of ego or a need to consolidate power, is a lonely and ultimately blinkered, even fearful leader. Good deciders are searching conversationalists, who learn from their associates. Which in turn allows them to better manage everything from office politics to personal insecurities. They "uncover concerns and considerations that are yet to be disclosed or hidden," Nutt writes. They are willing "to step into the unknown and remain there until true insight emerges."[35]

The capacity to sense what others need in order to perform better requires a certain quiet. And quiet is not necessarily comfortable. Quiet is unguarded. Undefended.

Few people have found the right words with his players more often than Steve Kerr, whose Golden State Warriors teams made five straight trips to the NBA Finals and claimed three titles from 2014 to 2018, and won a fourth in eight years in 2022. Kerr has a marked stillness in conversation, a habitual considerate tilt to his head. It's the physical expression of a listener, someone who is highly responsive, and not always preparing to speak. As impactful as anything Kerr says to the Warriors are his experiments with silence.

Kerr values the effect of silence so much that he runs a drill in it, called Silent 10. *Sports Illustrated*'s Chris Ballard once observed it in action: for ten straight minutes, the Warriors will mime their offense without a word spoken—running up and down the court using eye contact and hand signals only. Kerr's purpose with the exercise is to reawaken awareness of one another. It's an eerie few minutes, but it commands everyone's deep attention to what's going on with their teammates. When floor leader Stephen Curry wants to issue an order, he has to flash a fist and find a way to connect with the gazes of all four men on the floor.[36]

Kerr's point is that sometimes talking can be the dead opposite of clear, honest, open communication. When you talk too much you effectively silence or dominate other people. You may want to project an aura of verbal command, but that one-way communication actually shuts others down.

The NBA season is so long that words can become perfunctory

and Kerr can get sick of the sound of his own voice. Naturally, so do his players. That realization led him to another experiment in the 2017–2018 season. The Warriors were struggling to maintain their focus in the dog days of February and their action on the court had become rote. Kerr could hear the staleness in his voice. "I haven't reached them for the last month," he observed to the press. "They're tired of my voice. I'm tired of my voice."[37]

One Monday morning at practice he informed them, "You're going to coach yourselves." Kerr turned over the practice and game-planning to the players. Center JaVale McGee did the film session. He had to cut up video of that night's opponent, the Phoenix Suns, and lead his teammates through a discussion of what coverage to use.

That evening Kerr sat quietly on the bench as the Warriors got off to a sluggish start. They trailed 13–8 with seven minutes left in the first quarter when the first time-out came. In the huddle the Warriors looked at Kerr expectantly for instructions. Instead, he handed his clipboard to player Andre Iguodala. When he'd said they would coach themselves, he meant it. Kerr and his staff stepped aside while Iguodala convened the huddle and drew up some directions on the clipboard. Kerr didn't listen in. "That was the whole point," Kerr said afterwards. "It's up to them to communicate."

For the rest of the game the Warriors were noticeably more animated. In every time-out and huddle, different players took the clipboard. Steph Curry almost got a delay of game when he tried to draw up a play but put two guys in the wrong position. Eventually injured forward Draymond Green, in street clothes with a sprained hand, took command of the sideline. Kerr was delighted. The Warriors won by more than 40 points, 129–83. "They were passing the clipboard around and they were so invested in making those plays work," he observed later.[38]

The Warriors finished that season by running away with the NBA title.

A leader interested solely in the power of their own voice would never have tried it. But Kerr was more interested in what *they* needed to hear, not what he needed to say.

"A coach has to have the humility to ask for their input and the awareness that not every decision is going to pay off," Kerr says. "What makes decisions hard is that there is no easy answer. There are two angles to them. Number one is the angle of, how are my staff and I going to come up with a decision to a problem or an issue, and number two, how are we going to include the team? How is the team going to accept it? And those are equally as important."[39]

It's important to note, however, that too much silence has a double edge. Often, high performers will interpret silence as disapproval. "Here's one thing I learned, you always tell people how they're doing, even if it's someone like an MVP," Dungy asserts. "It's still good for me to say, 'You're doing a great job; you're doing exactly what we need to win.'"[40]

Pat Summitt once observed, "In the absence of feedback, people will fill in the blanks with a negative." They will assume that you don't like them, or that they're doing a bad job. Every coach knows this to be true from personal experience with players who became mysteriously insecure. Dungy learned this as a younger head coach in Tampa Bay in 1999 with a team that went 11-5 and won their division. One day his stalwart defender John Lynch said to him, "Coach, are we doing anything that you like? Are we any good at all?"

"Sure," Dungy replied.

"Well, we wouldn't know it," Lynch said.

Dungy was baffled. And then he realized that his silence had been taken as an implicit commentary. "I'm pleased, I'm fired up, they're playing great," Dungy remembers, "but they don't know it, because I haven't *told* them."[41]

The practical fact is that not all honest conversations are bonding. Some are confrontational—and some are severing. Then, too, not everyone receives words the same way: some hear praise as a whisper, and a directive as bullying. Especially in situations where there is an imbalance of authority. Coaches, like all bosses, can be decades older than their people, with a gulf between them and others in age, power, and security. What bridges those gaps is a leader's willingness to make himself or herself available to the exchange.

Kerr's ability to talk through problems with his team held the Warriors together when their easy inspiration was sorely tested by some tense internal conflicts. Power forward Draymond Green is a six-foot-six tower of broiling temperament, one of those chipped-shouldered, edgy athletes who can name every single player who went ahead of him in the NBA draft. Scouts didn't know quite what to make of him as college player at Michigan State because he didn't appear to be a great shooter and he wasn't quite big enough to meet the parameters of an inside player. The Warriors drafted him anyway because as Kerr says, "He's a winner. That's what position he plays."[42]

Green took some getting to know. He was clever, charming—and utterly tempestuous. He yearned to be great, yet when he felt suppressed or misused he would erupt in fury. Once, Green screamed at Kerr on the sideline in the middle of a game. Afterwards, when he tried to apologize, Kerr just said, "Nah, you're fine. I love your passion. Why would I try to stop that?" But at halftime of a 2016 game against Oklahoma, Kerr triggered Green when he barked at him for taking a shot instead of making the "right" pass to Steph Curry. Green went ballistic. In a profane fit overheard by an ESPN reporter standing out in the hallway, he screamed at Kerr, "You have me messed up right now!" ESPN ran a headline that announced: "Golden State's Draymond Green Problem."[43]

But Kerr genuinely didn't view Green as a problem. It was *his* problem—his job to learn how to manage the temperament of his most dynamic player—and Kerr took it on himself to attempt a rapprochement.

"I think part of coaching is trying to understand what each player is going through and thinking in his career, in a season, in a week, in a stretch, or even in a game," Kerr says. "And so you have to have that feel for who your players are and how they best respond, and what they might need to hear. And it's different for each guy."[44]

As both men described it to reporter Howard Beck of Bleacher Report, Kerr reached Green with a moving three-page letter that began: "I love and respect you. I know you're hurting." The rest of the letter essentially stated that when Green was at his best "we're at our best." But when he was at his worst "we suffer." Kerr's emotional honesty touched Green. "When you kind of see that out of somebody, you know it's not about what *they* want," Green remarked. The two men sat down and talked, and the more Kerr listened, the more he realized how much Green operated out of a furnaced sense of disrespect. When Green took a three-pointer instead of passing to Curry, he wasn't being selfish or heedless; he was saying, *You better start guarding me, motherfucker.* It was part of his competitive undergirding. Green *needed* to make some of those plays for his sense of self-worth. And by taking them away Kerr risked wounding his spirit.

"Draymond's made a big impact on me," Kerr confessed. "Because I've watched him go from second round pick . . . to All Star. And he's done it with intellect, versatility, and bravado. Without that bravado, Draymond isn't Draymond. So who am I to tell somebody, 'Hey, don't! Tone it back!' When maybe toning it up is what might help make you great."[45]

Their discussion didn't solve every problem overnight. Green remained a player who could dynamite a game, for good or ill. In 2018, Kerr had to suspend him for one game after he had an alpha confrontation with teammate Kevin Durant. When Green came back from the suspension he played terribly, going twenty-four minutes without scoring in a blowout loss to the Rockets. But their emotional honesty held. "I was horrible," Green admitted. Kerr said after the game, "We're banged up a little bit physically and right now we're banged up spiritually. . . . There is no getting around that. . . . Draymond may not have had his best night tonight, in fact he played very poorly. But I liked his approach. He was genuine out there." Genuine was the critical word. Despite their problems, the Warriors would make the NBA Finals for the fifth straight year.[46]

The notion that leaderly strength is incompatible with emotional candor is an increasingly useless old idea, but it's a tenacious one. In the fall of 2020, Dallas Cowboys quarterback Dak Prescott did a public service when he refused to follow the trope that a football player must never confess to any vulnerability.

In a video interview with sports journalist Graham Bensinger, Prescott spoke of losing his older brother Jace to suicide amid the isolation of the coronavirus shutdown and admitted that as a result, he himself had been struggling with a brutal compound of depression, anxiety, and insomnia and sought treatment for them. "I didn't necessarily know what I was going through, to say the least, and hadn't been sleeping at all," Prescott related.[47]

When the interview aired, it caused a sensation. A Fox Sports commentator named Skip Bayless reacted with a knee-jerk hot take, predicting it would undermine Prescott with the team. "The sport that he plays is dog-eat-dog," Bayless announced. "It is no compassion, no quarter given on the football field. If you reveal publicly any little weakness, it can affect your team's ability to believe in you in the toughest spot."[48]

Bayless was dead wrong. Prescott's confession redoubled his teammates' respect for him. "His ability to be transparent on his personal challenges that he's fighting through, I think is something that shows tremendous strength," his head coach, Mike McCarthy, said, "and I admire him for it." Even rival players from other teams congratulated Prescott for his courage.

It was an important lesson for any person—whether he or she wears a dark suit or sweats—who has felt worn out and unstrung. NFL football is no more or less hypercompetitive and compassionless than *your* daily life, and in thinking about how to deal with your no-quarter burdens, better to speak honestly. Asked if he felt compromised in any way as a leader by his admission, Prescott responded, "No, I think that is being a fake leader. Being a leader is about being genuine and being real."[49]

On the field, Prescott has been better than ever. In 2021, he threw a career-high thirty-seven touchdown passes. Clearly the Cowboys have no doubts about his leadership; their regard for him is expressed in a massive four-year, $160 million contract they awarded him. Not only has Prescott never regretted his confession; he has made it a habit to write "Ask4Help" on his wrist tape, visible during televised games.

Prescott demonstrated something vitally important about emotional candor: it's *the path to true strength*. Nobody makes this point more eloquently than the social worker–author and public speaker Brené Brown, who emphasizes it in her consultations with high-stakes performers, including NFLers who regularly seek her advice. Brown frequently visits military special forces and likes to relate the story of an experience she had at Fort Bragg. She asked a group of soldiers there a simple question. "Give me a single example of courage from your own life, or that you witnessed in anyone else's life, that did not require uncertainty, risk, and exposure," she said to the servicemen and -women.

Total silence.

Every single soldier in the room had felt vulnerable in trying to be brave. Her point: "Vulnerability is not weakness. It's our most accurate measure of courage."[50]

Prescott gave every player and coach in the NFL the permission to look at their own emotional landscape with candor. People who are able to do this become the most persuasive leaders—in all walks, not just on the field—because they are authentic, not just plastic-skinned, eggshell-egoed imitations of what they think strong is supposed to be. All of us must muster situational energies to get through hard days, but people who pose as impregnable are following a hollow mythology. It's not a sign of real fortitude. People, players, sense them as liars. Great leaders like Prescott have the interior security of knowing they have transparently *addressed* their weaknesses, not hidden from them. This enables them to cast a far mightier projection with others than they could otherwise.

The language of leadership has four basic characteristics: it is illuminating, not obfuscating; it is well structured to prevent misunderstanding; it is trustworthy; and it is emotionally connective, expressive. You know it when you hear it. Great deciders communicate from honest centers with ears for others and tongues that avoid blame, and this allows them to form powerful alliances.

Hear the tone of honest and kind inquiry in Bonnie Stoll's exchanges with Diana Nyad. Listen to the fundamental self-effacement of Steve Kerr in crediting his most complicated player, Draymond Green, for teaching him how to be more attuned. Consider the plainspoken gallantry of Dak Prescott's acknowledgment of his issues, which only deepened his team's belief in his underlying strength.

The right words have broader implications for us than just facilitating better decision processes in an office or workplace. They tell us a lot about whom we want to work for, and who we want our leaders and our problem solvers to be.

6.

Culture

The Environment

"Culture" is a word that can drive one crazy with its overuse and vagueness. It's the leader, just edging out "paradigm," for verbiage guaranteed to leave an irritability headache behind. What is culture, anyway? Its hazy usage results in any number of bumper sticker slogans on the walls of offices. Golden State Warriors coach Steve Kerr says, "We've all been in a gym where there's a big sign that says something like 'Only the Strong Survive.' And we're all, like, what does that even *mean*, right?"

The Latin root of the word, "cultura," means to grow or, literally, to till. Like anything that must be cultivated, it's an indistinct and somewhat mysterious process. "Unfortunately, in our experience it is far more common for leaders seeking to build high-performing organizations to be confounded by culture," wrote a team of analysts for the *Harvard Business Review* led by Professor Boris Groysberg. But what can be said with firm certainty is that it's about creating a healthy base atmosphere that nourishes success. You won't find that in any chief strategy officer's job description. But as Groysberg observes and Steve Kerr can affirm, "Culture eats strategy for breakfast."

"I think the biggest lesson I learned is that culture is way more important than scheme," Kerr said in a 2022 seminar with Harvard Law students and professors. "I would say coaching is maybe 25 to 30 percent strategy. Everything else is about communication and what your players feel when they come into the building every day."

Initially, Kerr thought building a winning team culture was all about scheme, tactics—he had strategies and points of emphasis, a million ideas. He had a plan. On the day he was named a first-time head coach of the Golden State Warriors in 2014, he brought a file of plays thick as a book to the job, accrued from his days as a player. He had been the beneficiary of great coaching throughout his pro career, won five championship rings under Phil Jackson and Gregg Popovich, the most illustrious names in the history of the game. "Nobody could ever ask for a better apprenticeship," Kerr observed. But for all of Kerr's deep background, his experiences had been with *other* people's locker-room cultures. He had never had to establish one himself.

Before Kerr started work, his agent suggested that he talk with Pete Carroll, the head coach of the NFL's Seattle Seahawks, a fellow client who had just won the 2014 Super Bowl. Carroll might have some advice about team building.[2]

Kerr spent two days in Seattle observing Carroll and the Seahawks in training and was awestruck by the dynamism of Carroll's organizational culture. Carroll had refashioned a perennial loser into a swashbuckling high-energy outfit, whose practices were so loud and fast-paced they seemed like dance parties. Music blasted from speakers, while players worked in drills with such an unbridled intensity that "they practically bounced," Kerr recalled.

At the end of the second day, Carroll invited Kerr to sit down and talk. He opened the conversation by asking, "So, how are you going to coach your team?"

Kerr replied, "Like, what offense am I going to run?"

"No, no, that stuff doesn't matter," Carroll replied, waving it away.

I've spent years trying to design an offense, Kerr said to himself, *and Pete Carroll just told me none of it matters.*

The x's and o's, Carroll said, were only a fractional part of running a team.

"Listen. Go back to your hotel tonight," Carroll told him, "and think about what the most important values are to you. And write them down. Who are you? What are you all about, and what are your uncompromising principles? What are you going to stand by, and what do you stand for?"

In Carroll's opinion, most inexperienced leaders didn't think hard enough about their personal philosophy of a workplace. They tended to go by conventional templates without really examining them. They focused on playbooks. Seldom did they take the trouble to think about the climate in which they asked people to work.

"Rarely have people sat back and said, '*These* are my choices. I do *this*,'" Carroll observed in a later exchange with Kerr, during the June 3, 2020, *Flying Coach* podcast on The Ringer network. "They don't sit back and evaluate, because they don't necessarily have to. But when you're competing on our level you've got to get stuff right, got to get your act together, got to know exactly who you are. You've got to know exactly what you're going to be giving these guys to help them be great."[3]

Carroll had learned this the hard way: as a young man he had been fired as head coach of the New York Jets after one brief season in 1994. Luckily, Carroll landed a job as an assistant with the San Francisco 49ers, where the Hall of Famer coach Bill Walsh still acted as a consultant and had an office in a back hall after retiring with three Super Bowl rings. Most of the people in the building were afraid to talk to the iconic, erudite Walsh. But Carroll began dropping by and quizzing Walsh, who in turn opened up to the younger coach. The things Walsh was most adamant about, Carroll told Kerr, weren't the particulars of his West Coast offense, but rather the underlying principles of creating a collective ethic.

A winning coach, Walsh believed, had to have "a conceptual blueprint." A philosophy that was "the aggregate of his attitudes towards fundamental matters. It is derived from a process of consciously thinking about critical issues and developing rational reasons for holding one particular belief (position) rather than another."[4]

Walsh had designed an entire organizational program for the 49ers, not just a schematic playbook, based in his fundamental conviction that for a team to be great, it had to bond. Every year, Walsh would call the team together in training camp and tell them, "The first thing we're going to do, before we run or play or have a practice, is integrate you as a team. Everybody is going to know each other." Walsh wanted to knock down any walls that might separate them, from race, to economic background, to religion, to geography. And he used every room in the building, from the laundry room to the lunchroom, to do it. Players tended to sit together in cliques in the cafeteria—especially the quarterbacks, who considered themselves the elites of the team. Walsh would make them move to other tables and intermix. As former 49ers quarterback Steve Young once observed, Walsh wanted his players to know one another "an inch or two" below the skin, so that when they were in tough circumstances they would act as a unified group rather than "as independent contractors."[5]

Walsh's influence moved Carroll to draft his own conceptual notions for a team culture. He spent hours writing his beliefs down, vowing that if he got another job as a head coach, he'd have a clear idea of what he wanted his team to look like, and why. He knew that he wanted to coach in a unique nonconformist way, with an emphasis on high speed and high energy. He wanted to explore ideas that some football traditionalists considered unconventional, enlisting performance psychology and neuroscience to help players "peak," and he wanted his organization to be cutting-edge in those areas.[6]

Carroll advised Kerr to go beyond the "systems" of the great, legendary basketball coaches he had played for. "What are the most important values to you," Carroll said. "Not to Popovich, or Jackson, or me, but *you*. Every person is different and unique to his set of circumstances."[7]

Kerr went back to his hotel that night and asked himself what his basic concept for Golden State was, what did he want it to be? All of the great coaches he had played for had varying brands of technical expertise. But that wasn't what really separated them, Kerr realized. It was that each of them had "a way to bind the whole group together," a unifying principle.[8]

What was his unifying principle?

All of us have at least *felt* culture, even if we didn't know what it was, in an unhappy or toxic workplace. In a losing culture, operations are balky, and underlings mistrust the deciders and even work at cross-purposes with them. Cynicism is the language, bad habit the custom.

So how exactly does a leader build a winning culture, in which people share high standards and give decisions credence?

The most distinct culture Kerr ever experienced was the one fashioned by Phil Jackson for the Chicago Bulls, for whom Kerr had played from 1993 to 1998, during their run of six NBA titles. By Jackson's own admission, he wanted to be far more than a coach but almost a Zen master in his dealings with players, to whom he taught meditation. His style of leadership was unapologetically about "moving the organization or culture of a group toward a higher nature."[9]

Every day started with a meeting in a team room filled with Native American artifacts, an expression of Jackson's deep interest in Lakota history, which he had acquired as a young man when he taught basketball clinics at the Pine Ridge, South Dakota, territory. Jackson referred to his team as "tribe" and explained the Lakota belief that in a tribe no one "acted apart" from the group.[10]

"It didn't feel like, oh man, we're having a team meeting," Kerr recalled. "It was just a gathering spot, and it started to generate conversation. We weren't necessarily going in there to establish some kind of fundamental that we were going to work on for our offense or our defense. We were just communicating. And it took me a little while to figure out what Phil was doing. But every day, that was the first part of our day—we were going to communicate. And that trust was being built up."[11]

By the end of their sixth championship season, Kerr recalled, "we had guys crying in front of one another in these meetings." Jackson had created an atmosphere of pure emotional honesty in player exchanges, "and it was never going to happen if he had said, 'Hey, we got a team meeting every Friday'. . . . This was a constant and it was a huge part of our culture, and it made everybody feel comfortable within it," Kerr observed.[12]

Jackson's culture was so all-encompassing that you couldn't separate his Triangle offense from it. The Triangle was an old movement scheme from the 1940s refined by Jackson's longtime assistant Tex Winter for the modern pro game, but in Jackson's hands it became something else, an entire ethic. Within the offense players formed a series of shifting, well-spaced triangles from one side of the floor to the other, passing and cutting until an opening was exposed in the defense. When run well it resulted in opportunities for all five players—and what Jackson called "Oneness" on the court. But Oneness wasn't "something you can turn on with a switch," Jackson said. "You need the right environment for it to grow."[13]

Sometimes Jackson coaxed his players into Triangle collaboration with music. He would play his beloved Talking Heads and tell his players how a team was like an orchestra, all playing different instruments but still "finding the melody and the rhythm and playing off each other," Kerr remembered.[14]

How well a team operated the Triangle depended on how unselfish its best players were, and how committed to Oneness. The precepts of the Triangle were almost religious to Jackson. They were not "Commandments," Jackson remarked, "but when one needs a standard of measurement it's as good as any I know." To make it work players had to surrender their egos—and the ball—so that the other team was continually perplexed by who might shoot. As Pat Summitt once said of the Triangle precept, which she learned directly from Jackson and Tex Winter, "You have to give something up to get something back."[15]

At times, it was so flowing and quick moving that it was almost a work of art. Jackson was an art and literature lover who gave his players some of the unlikeliest books, selecting them carefully for what might inspire them. Once he gave his players the poet's memoir *The Liars' Club* by his friend Mary Karr, about surviving childhood abuse and alcoholism to become an artist.

"Why in God's name would you have your perfect athletes read that book?" Karr asked him. "All it teaches is how to take an ass whipping, and you don't want them to learn that."

"It teaches courage," Jackson replied.[16]

It took courage to surrender personal armor and work together with different people, Jackson believed. "It doesn't matter how good individual players are—they can't compete with a team that is awake and aware and trusts each other," Jackson once said. "People don't understand that. Most of the time, everybody's so concerned about not being disrespected. But you have to check that attitude at the door—that defensiveness, that protection of your own image and reputation. Everybody needs help in this game. Everybody's going to get dunked on. We're all susceptible to falling down and being exposed. But when we lose our fear of that, and look to each other, then vulnerability turns into strength, and we can take responsibility for our place in the larger context of the team and embrace a vision in which the group imperative takes precedence over personal glory."[17]

Years later as Kerr sat thinking about Jackson's culture and making notes in his Seattle hotel room, he understood that it was inimitable. It was too personal, too idiosyncratic, and too eccentric for anyone else to pull off. If Kerr tried to talk about tribal Lakota culture and the Triangle, it would sound phony. He could not simply replicate that philosophy and expect it to work with the Warriors.

As Kerr went over his memories of the championship teams he had been part of, he did an exercise with himself. He literally verbalized, "What was I experiencing when I felt the strength of those cultures?"[18]

Under the great Gregg Popovich, winner of multiple Coach of the Year awards with the San Antonio Spurs, Kerr had experienced an intensely family-styled environment. "Pop's" culture was that of a benevolent patriarch presiding over a dinner table. He was authoritative on the floor—"The selfish player sits no matter what," he'd declare—but also a gentle questioner and listener, "almost like a good parent," Kerr observed.[19] Once, when one of his top players, LaMarcus Aldridge, demanded a trade, Aldridge thought Popovich would cuss him. Instead, Popovich took him to lunch, telling him, "I want to see what I can do to understand." By the end of the lunch, Aldridge decided to stay.[20]

Popovich wanted a locker room in which players felt emotional connections with each other and with the coaches. "You can only get so much satisfaction out of the ball going through the hoop," he once famously said. Popovich invited his players to be participants in decisions and not just pawns.[21] Sometimes he'd come into the huddle during a time-out and say, "What do *you* guys see out there?"

"And he was just as likely to use our ideas of what adjustment to make as his own," Kerr recalled. [22]

Popovich had not always been so empathetic. After graduating from the Air Force Academy, he'd done five years in the service from 1966 to 1970 before he became a coach, and in those days the norm was for a leader to be a dictator whose culture was based on fear. Coaching, as he saw it back then, consisted of drilling young men to the brink of physical collapse. If they got cramps, you fed them salt pills. "I was a wild man," he confessed years later on The Ringer network's *Flying Coach* podcast in a conversation with Kerr. He'd run players, "just killing them out on the court, maybe to show them I was tough, whatever that might be. We'd do the drills until their tongues were hanging out, and they had to repeat them and repeat them, and they had to be perfect. Then practice was over, see you later."[23]

But Popovich had a revelation: "That's really a shallow way to live. There's not a whole lot of satisfaction in that." He wanted a relationship with players. He wanted to care for them. The game was a grind, and they needed to be able to replenish themselves, both mentally and physically, and Popovich decided part of his job was to see to their overall well-being.

Popovich began to hold family-style dinners that became legendary rituals. He loved fine food and wine, with a passion that made him renowned in Michelin-starred restaurants. He would invite players' families to travel with them on the team plane and insist on eating a good meal all together, win or lose, after games. Meals were an indulgence when they won and a comfort when they lost, and in either case it was a pleasure to see the wonder on a young man's face when the popping of a cork and the scrape of a fork on a plate gave him a new sensory experience, a taste landing on his palate for the first time. When people ate together, they inevitably shared and became closer, more "interested in each other," as Pop said, and thus more collaborative.[24]

"It's a maturation process," Popovich reflected later to Kerr on *Flying Coach*. ". . . You realize how much more meaningful it is if you actually know about that player, or you can laugh with him. You can get on him, but he knows you're going to put an arm around him after practice, and then he's going to say, 'Well, this guy's crazy, but I know he loves me; I know he cares.' And then the satisfaction starts to grow. And then that's the Holy Grail, those relationships."[25]

The atmosphere that Popovich fostered was so centered around the players that when the Spurs won the 1999 NBA title and the stage was brought out for the trophy presentation no one could find him. Like a good father, he stepped out of the limelight. Most Valuable Player Tim Duncan was center stage wearing his new championship beaked cap and holding the trophy, but Pop was nowhere to be seen. Kerr finally spotted him: he and the rest of his staff were twenty feet off to the side. "Completely out of the picture," Kerr recalled. "And I'll never forget that because it was so symbolic of what he believed. 'This is your moment; you guys did all the work.'"[26]

Kerr's influences could not have been more different from one another, from the fastidious John Wooden, to the philosopher king Jackson, to the inquiring fatherly Popovich. Yet "they were all authentic to themselves, and they all had this beautiful culture they had built," Kerr realized. He now knew why Carroll had asked the question "How are you going to coach your team?"[27]

Kerr always performed best when he had the most fun. So, when he asked himself what he wanted the defining value of the Golden State Warriors to be, the word that came to mind, the value that he prized above all others on the basketball court, was "joy." Kerr wanted his team to feel the original pleasure kids do, when play is still just that, *play*. That would be his culture. And Carroll was right: that had absolutely nothing to do with x's and o's.[28]

But how does one go about building a "joyful" culture? Kerr's aim was to get Golden State's players to feel "a certain vibe" every single day in their working environment, not just occasionally. That would take more than a sign on a wall and a couple of sayings.

Before Kerr could impart his philosophy to the Warriors, before he could even convene a practice, he had to meet them. During the off-season Kerr flew all over the country to see every player at their home where they were most relaxed and comfortable. He even made a long-haul flight to see Andrew Bogut in his native Australia for a quick overnight visit. It was Kerr's first paving stone, a statement that established something central about his culture. "My philosophy is that it's the players' team," as Kerr would say later.[29] That he would spend thirty hours in the air just to have a two-hour dinner with his center made an immediate impression. The message was, *I'm willing to fly halfway around the world; that's how important players are to me.*[30]

"That to me is the first order of business for any leader in any field, to develop the relationship first," he said later. "Then you can lay out your vision, and talk about your plans, and what you have in store. Every person I've ever known responds to that human connection."[31]

When the Warriors convened as a team and Kerr made his opening statement, he didn't talk about himself. He talked about *them*. He didn't wave around his championship rings and declare he was going to whip the team into shape. He talked about how much he respected the talent in the room, and their accomplishments. The Warriors hadn't enjoyed much success in the playoffs, but they were a good squad that had won at least fifty games in each of the last two seasons, and they had the fourth-best defense in the league. Kerr believed they were ready to take off. "You've already built the foundation," he said. He was just there "to help you take the next step."

Only then did Kerr move on to what kind of strategy he wanted to employ—and he did so with a statement that electrified them. The Warriors had a deep roster, and he had thought a lot about how to use it. A loaded bench could be a double-edged sword if it wasn't managed right; too many discontented players competing for roles or minutes on the floor could curdle a team. Kerr wanted to involve all of them. "We're going to play everybody," he declared. On most teams, there were players who never saw meaningful minutes. But the Warriors would use their numbers to play fast and loose—and it was going to be joyful.

"That means one night it's going to be your night, and one night it's going to be somebody else's night," he told the room. "But if you let it happen, we're going to *roll* people. We're going to *overwhelm* them with our depth and our numbers. And if you do that, if you play fast and play loose, and have fun doing it every day, it can be an incredible run."[32]

And it was.

As the Warriors took the floor for their first practices, Kerr wanted them to *feel* the new culture, in every detail. "The values that are important to you have to come *alive*," Kerr observes. "And that's how culture is defined."[33]

His workouts began with warm-ups to pulsing beats that put something extra into everybody's step. Kerr assigned a young staffer to the task of making daily playlists so that the music was good, and current. "Otherwise, guys like me are going to play Hall and Oates," he joked. The music thrummed from the speakers as they skipped around, to Nelly's "Ride wit Me," Kendrick Lamar and Dr. Dre, and "I'm in Love with the Coco."[34]

Some teams warmed up in regimented lines. The Warriors' warm-ups began like a kids' free-for-all, with players casually throwing up any kind of shots they wanted amid the blaring music. Kerr joined in—at one point he *drop-kicked* a ball at the hoop, and it went in. People had to duck to keep from getting hit in the head.

Perhaps the most playful shooter in NBA history was guard Steph Curry. He entertained them with stunts, throwing the ball like a discus, or backwards from half-court. Pretty soon it became a thing. As Draymond Green marveled to ESPN, "The start of practice is a complete circus. Basketballs flying everywhere." The *New York Times* got wind of the spectacle and ran a headline: "For the Golden State Warriors, Practice Makes Perfect Silliness." It was everything Kerr wanted.[35]

They roared off to a 10-2 start, the best in franchise history.

Kerr knew from his own playing experience how leg-deadening and mind-wearying an eighty-two-game NBA season could be. It ran from October to June and spanned three full weather changes, from autumn leaves to dead-branch winter to summer blossoming. Kerr looked for ways to keep his guys fresh. He prioritized their sleep, ensuring players stayed overnight after road games so that they could get a full eight hours of rest. He took a page from Popovich and booked private rooms in good restaurants, for anyone who wanted to share a meal. That too became a thing. Ten or more players would go out to dine together, and they began doing it not by prearrangement but just because they liked to. "If it was McDonald's, we'd all be there, too," guard Shaun Livingston remarked to ESPN. They'd play uproarious games of credit card roulette for the bill.[36]

Kerr varied his approach at practices, to keep it interesting for players, so it still felt like a *game*. One day they arrived at the gym to find footballs instead of basketballs and ran around passing and catching. On another occasion they played baseball. Deep in the heart of February, the most grueling month, Kerr took them bowling. Often, he and Curry would end practice with free-throw shooting contests, riveting affairs in which they scored one another on the cleanness going through the net.[37]

To prevent meetings from getting stale, Kerr brought in speakers from far-flung professions to talk about their work. They heard from a special operations soldier, a Hollywood filmmaker, a community political organizer. "It's easy to get wrapped up in every game, every day, and one way to take the pressure off players is to talk about other stuff," Kerr believed.[38]

It got old watching game tape every day, so Kerr tried to put some eclectic mixes into their film sessions, surprising clips. Players would expect a scouting report on an opponent and instead old film of assistant coaches in badly dated haircuts would come up on the screen, and the room would explode in laughter.[39] Or he would splice in "things that might make sense from a totally different realm, that will be a great metaphor for winning a basketball game or just making the right play," he says. He was an admirer of Philippe Petit, the high-wire walker who in 1974 awed the world with his walk between the Twin Towers of the World Trade Center, balanced thirteen hundred feet above the sidewalk. There was no better lesson in concentration, Kerr believed, than the 2008 documentary on Petit, *Man on Wire*, so he screened it for them.[40]

They ran their record up to 42-9 with a club-record sixteen-game winning streak and were such a cohesive bunch that sometimes Kerr felt like he barely had to coach them. At one point they had the No. 1 offense in the league, led by two All-Stars in Steph Curry and companion guard Klay Thompson, nicknamed the Splash Brothers for their net-rippling three-pointers.[41]

"My goal by the end of the year is to just sit there and do nothing," Kerr remarked several months after that first season ended. "And that means it works. Because that's what a coach's job is. It's not to pull strings and call every play and direct traffic. It's to say, 'This is your team, here's the vision, and let's get to that point.'"[42]

The Warriors broke the NBA record for most wins by a rookie head coach and, as every basketball fan knows, routed their way to their first title in forty years, with a record of 67-15. Their coach was true to his word. They rolled people. It was the first of a run of three titles and five straight NBA Finals. And all along the way, they played like kids, like the game was just that, a *game*.

As Kerr demonstrates with Golden State, workplace culture is constructible. But like any other buildable endeavor, it's also prey to erosion or collapse if it's faultily made, with cheap or wrong components or a poorly laid foundation. What makes a culture strong and sustainable is the right match of materials, plans, and people.

Without fundamental "alignment" of those things, your organizational culture will be weak, Groysberg points out. It does no good to identify your workplace culture as "collaborative" if your reporting channel is hierarchical and inhibits fraternization. It's ridiculous to label your culture "innovative" and then hire play-it-safe veterans. There is no point in declaring that you have a "family" culture if your deciders are aloof. You can say you want a "meritocracy," but if you reward entrenched top execs with rich sinecures then you don't have a real culture.[45]

The NFL's Ron Rivera discovered how a basic misalignment could affect his culture as a first-time head coach of the Carolina Panthers. The son of a career military officer, Rivera set out to create a specific Special Forces ethos on his team, a culture of "hot wash" accountability in which his players could freely assess performance with coaches, the same way elite pilot crews or platoons conduct after-action reviews in which they hash out issues regardless of rank. Rivera was intrigued by military rites in which soldiers and officers throw their insignias into a circle in order to talk liberally and problem-solve. He wanted the same for his team. The problem was, no players would come into his office, much less talk.

Rivera's head coach's suite was up a flight of stairs, past a receptionist, in a sequestered hallway lined by other executive offices. His players were uncomfortable making the trip upstairs in front of all those upper-management eyes and ears. Finally, Rivera commandeered a cubicle area just off the players' locker room and shoved a small couch and a desk into it. "Instead of being secluded on the second story, I was downstairs and accessible, and it got to the point where some guys would come in to watch TV and have lunch or sit on my couch. I made myself available to conversations," he recalls.

Rivera would ask a player, "What do I need to know?" Relevant information began trickling in. Players confessed that his team meetings were poorly scheduled and organized—they started too early and lasted too long, which left the players tired and hungry and affected their effort on the practice field. "It's my fault, I'm the head coach," Rivera said after listening. "But if there are things I don't know, I need your help. You've got to tell me." When Rivera realigned his office layout and his practice schedules, he began to create the type of team he wanted.[46]

Look anew at organizations with indelible cultures, both sports and non-sports, and notice how their leaders align every detail. The New England Patriots complement Bill Belichick's "Do your job" mantra with their payroll strategy, filling the roster chock-full of effortful, undervalued, and workmanlike players. The Golden State Warriors and their "Splash Brothers" mentality are the result of Steve Kerr's commitment to exuberant playfulness in all facets—down to crazy shots in the warm-ups. Patagonia's "treat work as play" code has long been accompanied by founder Yvon Chouinard's convicted public environmentalism and willingness to hire adventurers over MBAs.

Patagonia is renowned for its high employee retention rate, and one reason is because the company's "do-good" culture is so closely married to its internal practices: 91 percent of its people call it "a great place to work" compared to the average of 59 percent at a typical American company. And when they're asked why, they all cite the same quality that Kerr does in establishing culture: authentic committment. There is no contradiction between its stated mission, actual business practices, and how it treats its employees.[47]

These are just a few examples of organizations that have their purposes, sensibilities, and structures in well-arranged synchronicity. *That* is culture.

When everything that attaches to an organization is bent to the same thematic end—mission, hierarchy, personalities, vocabulary, daily practices and rituals, even office décor—then you can create the powerful ongoing identity narrative called a "winning" culture. Groysberg and his colleagues identify four basic tools with which leaders can sustain this identity: 1. Articulate the character you aspire to, 2. make hires that reflect it, 3. communicate it across the organization, and 4. reinforce it with all of the structures and policies at your disposal, and without internal contradictions.

Tommy Amaker has performed one of the more striking acts of cultural realignment in all of sports in recent years as Harvard's head basketball coach. When he arrived at Harvard in 2007, a culture was already there, deeply engraved into the thick-stoned architecture. Even the buildings were deliberately designed to convey its solemnly restrained elitism, "a republican simplicity . . . and tempered freedom," according to an early architect.[48] The aged academic institution, which dated to 1636, was not only fully formed; it seemed immovable.

Amaker was the first black varsity head coach in the history of the prestigious institution. What's more, he was charged with completely remaking a basketball program on a campus that was strangely misaligned where sports were concerned. Harvard was the most ambitious institution in the country, yet deeply suspicious of athletic success. The university remained locked in a nineteenth-century conception of sports as "extracurricular." As Harvard athletic director Bob Scalise said, sports "would never be the sole reason that someone would be here at Harvard." Sports were seen not as part of the Harvard higher learning experience but as something that threatened to *interfere* with it.[49]

The irony was that this gave Harvard a peculiar tolerance for losing.

It was the only area in which the Crimson didn't strive to be elite.

That sensibility was visible in the basketball arena, a rickety old place named Lavietes Pavilion, which dated back to 1926 and had just a few bleachers that held two thousand seats. The Crimson had never won anything on that court. They were the only team in the modern Ivy League never to have won a conference title; nor had they ever beaten a single ranked team. That's how accepting Harvard was of losing.[50]

Behind his desk Scalise had a board listing the department's principles: "Adhere to the highest standards of integrity, ethics, and sportsmanship. Attract and develop people of outstanding capabilities. Grow and manage the department's resources wisely."

There was nothing on there about winning. Still, in 2007 Scalise decided it was finally time to upgrade men's basketball.[51]

Harvard's players were more than ready for the change. When Scalise asked the team leaders what kind of new head coach he should look for, they replied with an audacious suggestion: they wanted someone who could help them win something big. Namely, they wanted Tommy Amaker.

Scalise was taken aback. At first glance it was a total mismatch—and a totally unrealistic hire. Amaker had spent his whole life in the world of commercialized, win-obsessed, high-dollar, prime-time college basketball. He had been an All-American player at Duke, and won two national championship rings there in the 1990s as an assistant coach to his mentor Mike Krzyzewski. As a young head coach at Seton Hall, Amaker had sent players to the NBA and taken teams deep in the NCAA tournament. Most recently he had led superpower Michigan, which had a $160 million athletic budget, to three twenty-win seasons. He was a diamond-ringed, top-notch coach, for whom basketball was not a minor emphasis or academic distraction.[52]

For form's sake, to make his players happy, Scalise placed a phone call to Amaker. To his shock, Amaker agreed to meet for coffee. Would he even consider Harvard? Scalise asked.

He would.

When Amaker met with the Harvard search committee, one of the members, a former player named Tom Mannix, asked him with puzzlement, "Why would you want to come to Loserville, USA?"[53]

The answer was that Amaker had a nagging a sense of misalignment in his own career. Amaker had just been fired by Michigan despite averaging twenty wins a year, while digging the school out of deep mud. The program he inherited had been heavily penalized by the NCAA for breaking rules that forbade cash payments to players. Though Amaker restored both success and integrity to Michigan, he was nevertheless let go after just four years, simply because his team hadn't made it into the all-important "March Madness" NCAA tournament with its $220 million in payouts. Amaker was weary of the perpetual pressure to chase wins for the sake of athletic department revenues.

Amaker wanted to feel like a teacher, a faculty member. He was deeply attracted to Harvard despite its years of losing, he told Scalise and the search committee. He was from a family of teachers: His mother, Alma, had taught English in the Fairfax County, Virginia, school system for more than fifty years. Amaker was heir to a tradition in the black community that viewed the job of teacher "as a very, very *honorable* position," he recalled. "And I'm a product of that in a very honest way." He was so devoted to the craft that he would call up notable professors in the Michigan academic departments to ask about their instruction methods.[54]

"I'm a teacher and an educator first before I'm thinking about coaching," Amaker said of himself. "How that fits with anybody else, I don't care."[55]

Amaker didn't believe that winning big and teaching were incompatible. Duke had once been considered Loserville, USA, too, Amaker pointed out to the search committee. But Krzyzewski, with Amaker's critical help as his first big recruit, had turned a bottom-dwelling program into a perennial contender. Amaker himself was proof that quality basketball and higher learning could co-exist. He had gotten an economics degree in 1987 while making All-American as an undergrad and then gotten a master's from Duke in business while serving as an assistant to Krzyzewski amid their national championship campaigns.[56]

Amaker believed basketball had as much intellectual content as anything he had studied at Duke. In fact, Krzyzewski was the best professor he'd ever had, and that wasn't a knock on Duke's faculty. Too often, athletics were sequestered from other subjects. But what might happen if you actually stitched basketball to the rest of Harvard's culture, Amaker asked? He believed he could create a team that "befitted one of the world's great universities," he told the committee.[57]

A Harvard program that aligned both academic and athletic elitism would have a powerful double allure. It could be a home for people who wanted to be both "scholars and ballers," Amaker said. Harvard's workload could be an attraction rather than an obstacle—and his players could have an impact far beyond the dimensions of the court. His coaching would not be an extracurricular demand or distraction but a vital enhancement to it. "I have a responsibility to see my players not just as athletes but as future leaders, as well, so if I'm doing my job, they're going to be developing and learning and growing beyond the 94 x 50 feet," Amaker said.[58]

He was hired.

Not everybody met the description of scholar-baller. Amaker's first move was to follow Groysberg's advice that a leader must "select" people who meet the culture he's trying to build. Amaker caused a shock to the campus culture when he cut five players from the existing roster, recommending they join the junior varsity, to clear room for higher-quality recruits. Some in the Harvard community were appalled: they were accustomed to sports as a clubby recreation. But Amaker had no intention of trying to build a championship team with an inadequate roster.

Jeff Bezos has observed that you don't try to build a 747 out of your garage. "Unrealistic beliefs on scope—often hidden and undiscussed—kill high standards," Bezos once wrote to Amazon shareholders. "To achieve high standards yourself or as part of a team, you need to form and proactively communicate realistic beliefs about how hard something is going to be."[59]

Amaker was realistic: winning at Harvard was indeed going to be hard. He scoured the country for capable candidates who could meet the academic load. Brandyn Curry, from Charlotte, North Carolina, was an elusive point guard with a strong enough transcript that he won an offer from Stanford. Initially when Curry heard the word "Harvard," he asked his mother, "Do they even have a basketball team?" If they did, he assumed it was full of "nerds." But then Amaker visited him. Come to Harvard and be a "trailblazer," Amaker urged. Curry was nervous about it. "You're in class with all these people that could be the next president," he remarked to a hometown publication. But he committed.[60]

High-quality basketball had to be learned as attentively as any other subject at Harvard, Amaker stressed to his players. "We are not trying to get through practice, we are trying to get something *from* practice," he liked to say.[61] Amaker explained that his brand of Harvard basketball would be about more than just concrete strategy; it would embed a broader system of learning that would give players tools to deal with the tough inevitable competition they'd face no matter what their chosen craft or profession.

"We're going to be on so many more teams in our lifetime," Amaker observes. "Whether it's your church, some group in your community, where you work, your organization, your company. Even if you're an entrepreneur, you'll still have to work with others. And being on a team, God, that's a beautiful thing. Being on a team is to know what it means to be a tremendous teammate, and that is the game changer, to know what that encompasses, all the things that come within that context. The sacrificing. The role playing . . . To be a leader, you have to first show you can be a teammate. That's what *leads* you into becoming a leader."[62]

In film sessions, Amaker screened clips of great teams performing the actions he was trying to teach. He concentrated on a vision of the game as it could be played, rather than the less ideal product in front of him. "I believe in showing them how it *should* look," he says. "Showing them things done right, and saying, '*This* is how it's supposed to look, guys.'"[63]

The Crimson began to see a turnaround as doable. Winning, Amaker promised them, would be an inevitable byproduct of practicing and playing in a Harvard-worthy way. "We define our own success," he told them. "We're going to live up to our own internal standards." They went 8-22 in his first season, but in his second they broke even at 15-15. And in his third they went 21-8, the first time in school history they broke the 20-win threshold.[64]

Amaker's conviction that basketball was a valuable exercise "beyond the 94 x 50 feet" was bolstered by a core of faculty he met early in his tenure. Harvard Law School professor Charles Ogletree, a renowned social justice scholar, invited him to a breakfast with some colleagues in an effort to make the school's only black coach feel welcome. For a couple of hours over coffee and eggs, Amaker talked basketball and racial politics with Ogletree and a handful of other distinguished black professors. Amaker so loved the exchange—and the feeling of being a faculty member and not just a coach—that he asked if they could do it regularly.

"The Breakfast Club," as it became known, would convene monthly at Henrietta's Table, a restaurant in the Charles Hotel just off Harvard Square. A stream of brilliant personalities from across campus began to join them, and sometimes would bring notable guests, to converse about the intersection of sports and social justice. Massachusetts governor Deval Patrick came, and so did members of the Boston Celtics, and Kareem Abdul-Jabbar.[65]

It occurred to Amaker that his players needed to hear these discussions. *I should start bringing the guys*, he told himself. Pretty soon half a dozen ballplayers at a time were sitting around the table listening to some of Harvard's greatest minds. Amaker wanted his team to hear what these people could impart, "the walks that they walked," he said. His point to his players was: you are future leaders like these, and basketball is completely enmeshed with your larger education.[66]

The Breakfast Club was a crucial source of support for Amaker when the inevitable charges came that he and his players didn't belong in Harvard's culture. As Amaker brought in stronger talent and his team slowly but surely improved from its doormat status, the rest of the Ivy League schools didn't take it well. Other coaches charged Amaker with lowering university admissions standards to get players in. Amaker was livid. He insisted his players were well qualified and the only reason anyone questioned them was because they "looked different." In time, a six-month Ivy League investigation exonerated him: his recruits' academic profiles, test scores, and GPAs met Ivy standards, the report concluded. The charge that his players were unworthy along with an insinuation that he somehow compromised Harvard made Amaker seethe, but he used it as another excuse for teaching beyond the ninety-four feet. "Don't mistake visibility for importance," Amaker warned his players.[67]

The best revenge was to win—and the Crimson steadily won more year by year. By Amaker's fifth season in 2011, they were in the hunt for the Ivy League championship for the first time in school history. As the team stalked the title, Lavietes Pavilion became packed. Students clamored for victory in the old field house, until the noise rang off the metal struts in the ceiling. *Harvard Magazine* pronounced the hunt for an Ivy title "a sort of a holy Grail." It came down to a season-ending finale against Princeton on a Saturday night: a victory would assure Harvard of at least a piece of the title. The game was sold out, tickets were scalped for $300, and even ESPN took notice of the game. Harvard won 79–67, and as the buzzer went off, students stormed the court.

The sense of elation over accomplishing a first for ancient Harvard equaled anything Amaker had ever felt, at any level, in the game of basketball. As he remarked, "I'm not sure you can walk anywhere on this campus and find something that hasn't been done before."[68] Amaker had won a dual victory: he had proved good basketball players could be good students and good students could play good basketball.

But a larger cultural victory would be more elusive, the one in which young black athletes were regarded as the very best of a modern Harvard. It would be a continual challenge.[69]

The culture of Amaker's team became increasingly, explicitly activist. By the time of George Floyd's death at the hands of Minneapolis police in the spring of 2020, the Breakfast Club had swelled to more than forty members and needed a private room for their discussions about race and justice, with Amaker's athletes avidly listening in. Amaker took on race-education initiatives that he hoped would affect his future players: he campaigned to make African American history a required subject. "One of the reasons we're in the state we're in with racial justice is, we really don't know and haven't been taught the true history of our nation," he reflected. "We have never had the understanding, the teaching, the awareness, and ultimately the empathy of this nation, intertwined with African American history."[70]

Amaker's insistence that he could create "a team befitting of the world's greatest university" was inextricable from his fundamental understanding that there was no way to compartmentalize sports from the rest of American culture. No way to seal it off or partition it. When one of his newly graduated players, Seth Towns, was arrested at a George Floyd protest in Ohio just a day after completing his degree, Amaker declared that he was "proud" of him.[71]

Amaker's activism was accompanied by continued successes on the court. Amaker would lead the Crimson to seven Ivy League titles in fourteen years, with four appearances in the NCAA Tournament, a level of elite competition that had once seemed inconceivable.[72] Harvard even climbed into the Associated Press Top 25 rankings—the final point of arrival in college basketball.

But the ultimate ratification came from a player one graduation day. "I just wanted you to know that I've had a lot of coaches throughout my life as a player," the young man said. "But you're my only teacher." It was the most moving compliment Amaker had ever received. "It's what I always hope to be about," he says.[73]

By the fall of 2021, Amaker's incoming recruiting class was rated in the top fifty in the entire country. Former CEO Steve Ballmer was an enthusiastic booster, and one day Lloyd Blankfein, the former chief of Goldman Sachs, appeared on Bloomberg wearing a Harvard basketball shirt. Amaker had clearly achieved everything he set out to: a firmly entrenched basketball culture reflective of Harvard's reputation for intellectual quality.

"The culture's been derived through a lot of moments and layers," Amaker reflected. "It's the trust, the confidence you have in the way a team is constructed, that translates into winning. There are times when you have all that and you *don't* make the shot, and lose the game. But that doesn't mean you haven't created a situation that was incredibly positive and healthy. And over the long haul, the long course of a season or the long course of a career, you will do better than not because of the way you have tried to construct the environment."[74]

7.

Failure

The Teacher

Every year on the field of the Super Bowl, there are as many players who were once considered failures as there are bits of victory confetti. They're everywhere you look: drifters and discards, guys who have been cut, or traded, or lowballed before they found their way on to a winning team. In 2020, the champion Kansas City Chiefs had twenty-seven players on their roster who were not even chosen in the NFL draft.

Four inches. That was the margin by which, a year earlier, the Chiefs had suffered one of the most anguishing failures in NFL history. In the 2019 AFC Championship Game, they had fought for three hours against the New England Patriots, through dramatic back-and-forth switchbacks in momentum. Finally, they held a 28–24 lead with just fifty-four seconds left. For one fleeting moment, it appeared that they had won the game when they intercepted a desperate pass from Tom Brady.

But there was a yellow penalty flag on the ground. A Chiefs defender named Dee Ford had set up in an illegally aggressive posture offsides—by four inches.

Four inches. It was an infinitesimally small failure. Dee Ford was incredulous on the sideline. "They said I was offsides! Was I??" He was—film replay showed it—by four inches.

The penalty for the four-inch mistake negated the interception. The Patriots went on to win in overtime and reach the Super Bowl. While the Chiefs went home, choking on their disappointment.

The Chiefs could have been incensed at the pettiness of the officiating call. Or they could have blamed Ford for the loss. But head coach Andy Reid took a different tone. He told the team, "We all could have been four inches better. We've got to move forward."[1]

For the next year, Reid made "four inches" the Chiefs' mantra. Every day, they worked for a few millimeters of improvement.

The result? A year later the Chiefs were the victors in the Super Bowl, defeating the San Francisco 49ers by 31–20—after fighting back from a 10-point deficit in the fourth quarter. Asked after the game to identify what quality had carried his squad to the title, Reid replied that everyone had simply decided to get "four inches better."

"They put their mind to it, as did the coaches, and everybody upped their game," Reid said. [2]

Winning coated all they had been through with a false patina. The shine on the sterling trophy in Reid's hand distracted from the unspectacular truth, an invaluable axiom of use to any person trudging through difficult circumstances: If you want to turn events around, you can never underestimate the value of your past failures.

Show me a championship team and I'll show you a roster full of desperadoes. In January of 2021 it was the Tampa Bay Buccaneers' turn to win the Super Bowl. Of their fifty-three-man roster, they carried twenty-two members who had been rated as just two-stars or less in high school by talent evaluators. In other words, almost *half* of the members their championship squad once looked like every other skinny reject on a field.

New York Giants head coach Brian Daboll has a novel way to vividly illustrate the value of failure, according to ESPN. Once, as an assistant coach with the Buffalo Bills, Daboll opened a team meeting by asking every player and coach in the room to stand up. Then he said:

"Any coach who has ever been fired, sit down."

Every coach in the room sat.

"Any player who has ever been cut or traded, sit down."

Three-quarters of the men in the room took a seat. Now just a few men were still standing.

"If you weren't picked in the first round of the draft, sit down," Daboll said.

The rest of the players sat. All but one. The only man left on his feet was their quarterback, Josh Allen.

Daboll then said to Allen, "Josh, how many college scholarship offers did you get out of high school?"

"None," Allen replied.[3]

"Sit down," Daboll said.

Now the whole room was seated. And everyone knew that winners aren't born; they are made—and they are made out of people who have been losers at one time or another.

The question haunts every decision-maker: What if I fail? Consequences may be the single most hesitancy-inflicting factor faced by someone trying to make important choices. Fear both is personally paralyzing and leads to organizational inertia. But elite sports competitors have learned what an entire field of psychologists would love to be able to teach: how to persist professionally in the face of failure without losing your fundamental confidence.

The management scientist Paul C. Nutt has estimated that literally half of all organizational decisions fail. His analysis found a striking difference between corporate leaders who are able to break out of a failure mode and those who compound their mistakes. The successful ones are more forthright and searching when a decision goes wrong. They treat losing with a spirit of inquiry. Like Andy Reid, they look deeply into their own processes for its weak points.

Reid's central insight after that four-inch loss was that organizational failure is always more complicated and collective than a single individual hapless mistake. He refused to scapegoat Dee Ford or the officials, and instead led his team in a frank interrogatory about how to get better across the board. He engaged in Nutt's open "discovery process" and insisted that *all* the factors involved in the failure be fairly analyzed and worked on.[4]

Leaders who choose denial or blame shifting in the face of setback tend to stay stuck in failure mode. Show me a team that complains about officiating and I'll show you one that is likely to lose again next year, too. Doormat teams are those whose leaders seek convenient answers and shallower processes, grab the first easy explanation, and thus multiply the original missteps.

In business, this cycle can sometimes lead to massive exposure. Nutt cites the Firestone disaster of the 1990s as an example: Radial tires installed on popular Ford SUVs were separating and curling like snakeskins in hot weather, causing the cars to veer all over the highways and in some cases flip. At first, executives at both Firestone and Ford denied there was a major design issue and declined to do recalls, deeming it too expensive. After more than eleven hundred accidents, Congress convened hearings on the matter. In the end the cost was in the billions.[5]

Nutt's interest in massive corporate "debacles" led him to identify some "best practices" for dealing with failure. The best practice of all, Nutt asserted, is to resist hindsight bias and "recognize a richer set of possible causal events."[6] Good deciders ask, What was an avoidable mistake, and what was a reasonable or even acceptable failure? What was pure coincidence? Where was the competitor simply better? They recognize the uncertainties, pressures, and urgencies of the moment that affected the outcome.[7]

As Nutt observes, "Hindsight requires little imagination and allows a critic to trumpet a now clear-cut relationship of cues and consequences." But that clear-cutness—while it may be reassuring cover—is deceptive. In hindsight all the uncertainties have been "washed away," which results in misleading conclusions.[8]

It's counterintuitive, but good decision-makers make a certain amount of failure discussable, and even permissable. In any dynamic exercise, there will inevitably be some "misses," because you're asking people to make bold choices and enact them with high commitment.

"You have to be willing to get booed," as former Duke football coach David Cutcliffe puts it.

Intolerance of failure leads to hesitancy. Leaders who expect every decision to be a winner will wind up with teams that tend to freeze in "the clutch." Such leaders create a "perverse incentive" to bury information, according to Nutt. People begin "to scurry about taking defensive action," producing reports or rationalizations that cloud the truth. Which leads to what Nutt aptly terms "shrouded outcomes." Again, cover-ups.[9]

The best athletic play callers recognize that all of their best and worst decisions come with complexities and ambiguities that require deep dissection. The ultimate fallacy about the "right call" is that there is such a thing in every instance. Ask Steve Kerr of the Golden State Warriors about his "right" and "wrong" calls, and he replies that it's absurdly reductive to dwell on whether one play can determine a game.

"I don't think it's that simple," Kerr reflects. "It might be I made all the right decisions and a guy missed a shot. But the reverse might be true, too. I could have completely butchered a game, and then Steph Curry made six threes in a row, and we won. So I think that's too clean of a question for something that's so gray."

He continues: "The number of times you truly impact the result based on a decision you make during the game, a strategic one, a substitution, or a play call at end of the game, those are actually rare. Every once in a while, you draw a good play at the end of the game, and they score and you feel good. Or vice versa."[10]

The "vice versa" happened to Kerr in a game in November of 2019. It was a long, hard slog of a season in which the Warriors were decimated by injuries. In the final fifteen seconds of a contest against Charlotte, the Warriors trailed by just a point. Kerr had to decide who to put on the floor for the final sequence. Charlotte was at the foul line with guard Terry Rozier, a player who makes an average of 85 percent of his shots from there. The likelihood was that Rozier wouldn't miss, so there would be no rebound. Kerr decided to pull his biggest player, center Willie Cauley-Stein, out of the game and instead he put the Warriors' quickest shooters on the floor, in the hope that they could streak up the floor after the free throws and try to tie it with a three-point shot.

But then the unlikeliest thing happened—Rozier missed *both* free throws. The rebound caromed off the rim—and into Charlotte's hands because Kerr didn't have a big man on the floor to go up and get it. The Warriors lost. "And I didn't sleep that night," Kerr says. "I beat myself up."[11]

What helped Kerr finally sleep was placing the failure in its proper context, something he strives to do for his own players. Kerr spent the early part of his own NBA playing career tied up in knots over the pressure of taking clutch shots. He feared missing—but couldn't talk to anyone about what he felt because the NBA alpha ethos at the time was that players didn't dare confess that they weren't confident. The last thing Kerr was inclined to say to the head coaches who controlled his playing time was, "Hey, man, the hoop looks like a thimble to me right now." When the designated shooter secretly dreads the shot and lacks confidence, how is any coach's play call supposed to look very smart?[12]

Kerr finally became a deadly clutch player when, ironically, he accepted that a certain amount of failure was inevitable and gave himself over to it. "Probably the biggest lesson I learned during my career was finding outcome independence—that was really the key to performing under pressure," Kerr has observed. "You have to be willing to fail."[13]

Statistically, even the greatest shooters in basketball miss *well over* half the time. Take LeBron James, the most dominant player of his era: as of 2021, James had a clutch shooting percentage of 41.6 percent in the final 120 seconds of games, a greater decisional-failure rate than most of Nutt's corporate leaders.[14]

Everyone should have the outlook of James after a really bad day at work. In Game 3 of the 2013 NBA Finals, James flatly embarrassed himself. He missed fourteen of twenty-one shots he took against the San Antonio Spurs as his team lost. "I played like shit," he acknowledged frankly the next day at practice. But then he added. "As dark as it was last night, it can't get darker than that. I guarantee I'll be better tomorrow, for sure." And he was. In the final two games of that series, James threw down thirty-two and thirty-seven points respectively and hit the critical basket that led to a championship. What made James able to respond to an embarrassing loss so effectively? His ability to embrace failure.

The next time you're tempted, as a viewer, to criticize James for missing a game-ending shot, consider this: James may miss. But he has taken more clutch shots than any of his NBA peers over his twenty-year career. He never shies, never opts out. He's willing to shoulder the responsibility, to put himself in the hottest spot, again and again.[15]

A game-ending shot requires several calculated decisions in a matter of fractional seconds—what kind of shot, where to take it from, exactly when to let it go. Consequently, a miss necessarily leaves lots of room for second-guessing and blame of the shooter. Especially if you spend too much time on social media platforms reading the comments of pure bystanders.

"You're *vulnerable*," Kerr has observed. "Right? You put yourself in a position where you're going to be judged by millions of people watching. All of your athletes are out there laying it on the line. And there's so much at stake. And even as coaches we feel that, right? Every move we make is being watched . . . all of a sudden, you're in this microwave. And to me how you handle both the winning and the losing aspect as a coach is really crucial."[16]

Kerr wants his players to have what he calls "delete buttons," to erase the failure once it's processed and start again. It's an outlook that was best articulated by Kerr's childhood hero, John Wooden. "Losing is only temporary and not all encompassing," Wooden said. "You must simply study it, learn from it, and try hard not to lose the same way. Then you must have the self-control to forget about it."[17]

To Kerr, the definition of success in the clutch is not about the make or the miss. Success is being willing to *take* the shot. What matters, Kerr muses, is finding the courage to keep firing, without fear or vanity, in the face of the probabilities.[18]

"Nobody can win every game and makes every shot, or makes every decision right," Kerr says. "And it's never been more difficult than it is these days with all the judgment and the criticism. But there is such great value in going for it, in putting yourself in the moment, and not fearing the repercussion of the miss, or the loss."[19]

Athletes tend to be more resilient in the face of failure than the rest of us because they grasp an essential fact: you can't improve something until you've stressed it.

In 2009 two researchers from the University of Pennsylvania, Jonah Berger and Devin G. Pope, asked the question: "Can losing during a competitive task motivate teams and individuals . . . to perform better overall?" They analyzed more than forty-five thousand college basketball games and eighteen thousand NBA contests and found that trailing slightly at halftime actually led to an increase in winning percentage. NBA teams that trailed by small margins won at about a 6 percent higher rate. Why would this be? They respond to reversals with intelligent adjustments.

Simply put, champions are good losers.

They have the minds of engineers in this respect. Kevin Kelly, the founding executive editor of *Wired* magazine, once observed in an essay titled "The Virtues of Negative Results" that "great engineers have a respect for breaking things that sometimes surprises non-engineers, just as scientists have a patience with failures that often perplexes outsiders. But the habit of embracing negative results is one of the most essential tricks to gaining success."[20]

In the same vein, chairman Jeff Bezos has long championed failing as a fundamental virtue at Amazon. "Failure comes part and parcel with invention," he wrote to his shareholders. "It's not optional."[21] Bezos wanted his staff to do a lot of "wandering," which meant there would necessarily be some ideas that didn't work, and some that would initially seem absurd. For instance, "No customer was asking for Echo," he once observed. "If you had gone to a customer in 2013 and said, 'Would you like a black, always-on cylinder in your kitchen about the size of a Pringles can that you can talk to and ask questions, that also turns on your lights and plays music?' I guarantee you they'd have looked at you strangely and said 'No, thank you.'"[22]

No individual in business has arguably failed more often than Amazon's founder. The Fire Phone was a terrible failure, costing the company hundreds of millions. So was Pets.com, an early experiment in ecommerce retailing that went to liquidation in just 268 days, taking some $300 million in venture funding with it. The failure of LivingSocial cost another $175 million. "I've made billions of dollars of failures," Bezos remarked at one point. "Literally billions of dollars of failures." A few big successes, such as Amazon Web Services, Kindle, and Amazon Prime, offset the "dozens and dozens of things that didn't work." The smaller failures were worth it, Bezos believed, because they helped Amazon avoid the biggest failure of all, becoming obsolete in a fast-moving field. He has even bragged, "I believe we are the best place in the world to fail (and we have plenty of practice!)."[23]

Persistence in the face of failed (and even ridiculed) experiments does not mean head banging. As with Nutt's corporate deciders, there is a critical difference between engineers who deal with a failed trial in an coherent way and those who rashly tear things up or stubbornly dig in. According to a 2019 study, "Quantifying the Dynamics of Failure across Science, Startups and Security," that appeared in *Nature*, successful tech start-ups had a method for making *well-directed* modifications to their initial failures. The authors looked at failure data across forty-six years of ventures and concluded that the eventual succeeders had made "critical refinements to systematically advance towards success." Whereas those who repeatedly failed reacted in a disjointed, unorganized way.[24]

In short, great leaders fail with a more organized sense of purpose.

As any coach can tell you, game strategists who refuse to experiment will eventually find themselves in a desperate position against faster and more innovative competitors. Playing it safe, ironically, over time, may require ever-greater gambles with higher probabilities of failure. Bezos observes that those who don't innovate can wind up having to make a "bet-the-whole-company decision" akin to a sports Hail-Mary pass to save themselves.[25] It's counterintuitive, but chronically conservative decision-making can eventually force you into ever-more-uncomfortable risks.[26]

The best coaches thus have a tolerance for uncertainty as they restlessly experiment and remake their teams—changing lineups, strategies, rosters. They abhor stagnation, because they know that to stand pat is to be left behind.[27]

Not many coaches have committed to experimentation—and courted more controversy—than former U.S. women's World Cup soccer coach Jill Ellis did from 2014 to 2019. Ellis had arguably one of the most pressured coaching jobs on the planet: she had to totally revamp an iconic team for whom winning World Cups and Olympic gold medals was not an achievement but a mere expectation. "Target's on the back. . . . Anything less is considered a failure in everyone's eyes," as player Carli Lloyd said.[28] Over a five-year span Ellis repeatedly flirted with failure, in the name of growth.

"I got heavily criticized externally and even internally," she says. "It becomes hard. But you lean on the big picture of what's best for the program. That's what leads you through the tough conversations and the criticism. . . . You have to make the decision that you can live with it if it goes wrong."[29]

Ellis left a comfortable post at UCLA, where she led her team to eight Final Fours, to assume a seat that there was nothing comfortable about. As the USA coach she was in charge of a roster loaded with headstrong personalities like Megan Rapinoe, Hope Solo, and Abby Wambach, players who were skeptical of authority by tradition. They had battled for resources in a historically sexist sport, been toughened by living up to their own world-dominant standard year after year, and run off more than one head coach. They were also an aging team struggling with staleness, and required extremely delicate handling.

In the 2016 Rio Olympics, they suffered a disastrous quarterfinal loss to Sweden. It was the first time in program history they hadn't made it to the gold medal match. The loss was compounded by wounded pride over the fact that Sweden was led by their former coach, Pia Sundhage, who had resigned to return to her native country. Sundhage knew the USA's weaknesses intimately, and she designed a slow-paced, conservative game plan she knew would stymie them. It enraged the USA's most volatile member, goalkeeper Solo, who called the Swedes "cowards" in the postgame press conference.

Ellis decided it was time for a wholesale reconstruct. The rest of the world had caught up to the Americans in speed and technical skill, and they needed an infusion of youth and new tactics. They had to evolve with a younger, more versatile group that could adjust to different styles of play, "A team that could problem-solve within the game, that would have more tools," she says. It would necessitate a long period of acclimation and experimentation with different lineups. And it also meant there would be some unaccustomed losses and controversies.

"If you become static, you're dead," Ellis says. "What I felt coming out of the Olympics was, we've got to have a more fluid environment; some have to go, and some new players have to come in. We've got to have a new identity. Change *had* to be a part of it."

Ellis started by not renewing Solo's contract. With Solo's exit and the retirement of some other longtime stalwarts, "I blew up the hierarchy of the team," Ellis recalls.[30]

Players didn't know if they were starters or nonstarters. Ellis even left a captaincy open. She consigned Carli Lloyd, whose three goals had clinched the 2015 World Cup, to the bench, a move that bitterly discontented the star. The sheer churn and demands of adjusting to new roles created predictable tensions on and off the field. They lacked cohesion as they tried to make tactical transitions, and when they suffered two uncharacteristic upsets in the 2017 season, a group of frustrated veterans went to the United States Soccer Federation, and demanded that Ellis be fired if she didn't address their concerns about the roles and direction of the team.

But the head of U.S. Soccer, Sunil Gulati, sustained Ellis and told them that she wasn't going anywhere. Ellis was unfazed by the confrontation. Her father, John Ellis, a former Marine Royal Commando from England and a longtime soccer coach, had early on in her career given her two valuable pieces of advice. She had to be willing "to be fired, because that's part of the job," he told her. And she had to be willing to be unpopular. "Fifty percent will be with you, and fifty against," he said.[31]

To find the versatility the USA needed meant Ellis had to try out as many player combinations as possible. She called up a total of sixty different players to camps and tryouts, a number that signaled just how serious she was about wholesale turnover, given there were just twenty-three available roster spots. Which in turn compounded the number of difficult decisions she had to make—and the number of players she had to have blunt conversations with, and who second-guessed her. "When you're selecting A over B, it's open to scrutiny, and it's constant," she remembers.[32]

It was the harder way to do it. As Nutt has observed, many leaders default to status quo decisions, because "it provides instant relief for decision makers." Ellis sought no instant relief as she sorted through and discarded various lineups. The questioning of her tactics and lineups would continue through the remainder of her tenure, and endurance in the face of unpopularity was one of her most underrated feats.[33]

By 2019, Ellis had refreshed the roster with eleven new players who had never appeared in a World Cup. The roster's mix of newcomers with fresh legs and celebrated veterans was powerful. Some discontent lingered, but Ellis told them firmly, "Mission matters most. Put all your shit aside." They came into the World Cup tournament on a roll with nine straight victories—and in seven of them, they held opponents scoreless. As defender Kelley

O'Hara said later of Ellis's experimenting, "It wasn't easy. It was hectic and stressful and difficult and full of obstacles and a lot of uncertainty for a lot of people, but it was necessary, and I respect her a lot for doing that."[34]

The 2019 World Cup, staged in France, required seven games in a month and the USA would have to defeat the home team in Paris to get through to the final. Complicating the pressures were matters of politics: Rapinoe had gotten into a Twitter war of words with President Donald Trump, and the players were in the midst of an unresolved equal-pay lawsuit against their federation. But the team sailed through it all with a breathtaking virtuosity. Ellis used every single player on the roster in the earliest stages, spreading the glory around and building their confidence. She even kept team captain Alex Morgan on the bench as a reserve in a game against Chile. Critics wondered if she cost them some rhythm, but Morgan defended Ellis. "There was really no explaining to do," Morgan said. "I feel like this team has incredible depth, and when she chooses who goes on during the game, and who starts, there's no explanation needed. We trust in her."[35]

The second-guessing of Ellis never really stopped. But most of her moves visibly paid off. The USA was a marauding team with endless variety that made them almost impossible to defend. They scored twenty-six goals while giving up just three in the entire tournament—it was the most dominant the USA had ever been on the pitch.

"How do you live with ten million people criticizing your decisions?" Ellis asked rhetorically months later. "At some point I'd say to myself, 'Everything at this point, and this moment, has prepared me. And I'm the person that knows the most.' You have all the information. The media, and even your players, don't have all the info. You have to trust your information and be guided by it, because you see the whole iceberg, and most people just see the tip."[36]

Ellis operated from a simple conviction: if the USA team failed, she at least intended to fail in the right way. "You have to be able to live with a miss," she says. That attitude, more than anything else, allowed her one of the greatest victories in the team's illustrious history.

Some mistakes are irreversible, and some losses can't be recouped. What then? How do you live with a decision that leads to a very visible and permanent failure?

Know why you did it. When you have engaged in a good "discovery process" and understand yourself and your own thinking, failure is bearable. Can you be proud of the job you did and the way you conducted yourself, even if others measure the experience as unsuccessful?

There is a broad recognition at the top tier of the sports world that almost nothing happens the way you would wish it to. Competition is protean, with constantly shifting factors in a fog of action, including bad luck, unforgiving circumstances, and sometimes unstoppable adversaries. What matters most is how you respond. Do you admit your mistakes, appraise events candidly, and use the setback as a setup for a better result next time?

As a young football coach in his first head job with the Carolina Panthers, Ron Rivera tended to balk in fourth-down situations with win-loss consequences. The calls were so heavily scrutinized that Rivera, like a lot of NFLers, was risk averse, and it led him to an especially tormenting loss during the 2013 season. Rivera's Panthers led the Buffalo Bills by 20–17, with possession of the ball. They just needed a couple of yards to keep alive a drive, to consume the clock and clinch the contest. Instead, Rivera elected to play it safe and kick a field goal. But it was an utterly meaningless three points. All it did was give his team a six-point lead. That did nothing to put the game out of reach—a touchdown by the Bills could still beat them. Which was exactly what happened. Rivera's caution cost his team their momentum, and the Bills promptly drove the length of the field to score a touchdown, and handed the Panthers a one-point defeat.

Afterwards, Rivera decided to do some tough self-analysis. He sought out John Madden, the legendary former coach for the Oakland Raiders and broadcast analyst, for a critique.

"What could you have done differently?" Madden asked him. Rivera acknowledged he could have tried for it on fourth down, but "I was just going by the book." Madden just looked at him and said, "Ron, what book? Use your guts and experience."

The conversation totally altered Rivera's thinking. Leaders have to commit without quaking, Rivera decided. He could live better with a loss if it came from a committed decision to go all-in, than a hesitant, weak "by the book" rationale based in fear of failure.

"You think about consequences," Rivera says now. "There are two sets of consequences, right? Positive consequences. Negative consequences. In my experience, the more you think about the negative consequences, the more often you make a bad call."[37]

Rivera discovered something interesting when he became more committed in his play calling: His players committed with him. When they saw his willingness to make a hard decision without fear, they redoubled their effort to make the play work. It was a human factor that no probability calculation or data analysis could account for. In a one-month stretch, Rivera went for it on fourth down three different times—and the Panthers converted all of them. On each occasion he told himself, "If we can do it here, we can keep it rolling." When the players came to the sideline, they told him, "Thanks for believing in us, Coach." His dynamic quarterback, Cam Newton, said something that Rivera would never, ever forget.

"Coach, if you make that fourth-down call, I can promise I will do everything in my power to make it work," Newton told him.[38]

No one has more reason to fear career repercussions from their decisions than professional coaches and athletes. They are dogged by the specter of being fired. The average career length for an NFL player is somewhere between 2.5 and 3.5 years. Few of them have guaranteed money in their contracts, and every year their skills are appraised for deterioration. The NBA is hardly much better, with an average career of about five years.

Coaches are no more secure than their players. A 2019 survey of pro coaching job security over twenty years found the following: NBA coaches were the most vulnerable to firing, replaced on average every 2.4 seasons, while the National Hockey League was next at 2.6 seasons and Major League Baseball was third at 3.1 seasons, while the average NFL tenure was 3.2 seasons.

Yet that wasn't the most significant finding. The survey also discovered that teams with less turnover tended to have better records. Those with the most turnover annually tended to have records below .500. Probably because their owners made rash decisions and jettisoned people prematurely, with low tolerance for failure.[39]

Fortunately, most decisions don't have such immediate dire career consequences for the rest of us. Still, the struggle to make good daily choices in our worlds can feel like a profoundly consequential battle—questions can seem heavy, and the outcomes irrevocable. We're all connoisseurs of heartbreak. Each failure or loss is its own brand of pain.

In the summer of 2021, *Washington Post* editors recognized the burdensome effect the coronavirus epidemic was having on our daily decision-making, the degree to which it had complicated and pressurized everyday choices. They published a useful essay titled "How to Deal with Regret and Forgive Yourself for Making Imperfect Decisions." In it, a psychologist named Tara Brach noted, "Self-blame shuts down learning centers in the brain."

Some remorse is useful if it leads to thorough, hindsight-free analysis, but too much can lead to blindness instead of helpful realization. A Marine Corps major named Thomas Schueman, who teaches courses on "moral injury" at the Naval Academy and helps leaders deal with the attendant guilt of command decisions, told the *Post*, "Real tragedy is when you don't find meaning in your mistakes."[40]

By now it should be apparent that the "right call" is not a single declarative command issued by a maestro. It's a composite— of informed calculation, consultation with others, and a handful of good fundamentals in execution. Even then, it may not work. There are simply "grays" in decisions, especially at the head of complex organizations. Uncertainties and shifting urgencies can affect "the right call," and no decider always gets justice or is in full control of their fate. What matters is to sort through events, truthfully, with accountability from yourself and others, to discern what was an avoidable mistake, as opposed to a reasonable failure. Then you can live with the result and move on.

It's an age-old question in sports: Do you learn more from winning or losing? Maybe the reason we have such a hard time arriving at a definitive answer is that we view them as separate experiences, instead of as related. The truth about winning and losing professionally is that neither has much value by itself. If you lose all the time, it becomes a bad habit, and if you win all the time, you develop overconfidence and a narcissistic tendency to assume you are superior. What makes a worthy decision-maker is the ability to see the winning and the losing as deeply intertwined and equally valuable. This is what enables us to lose without losing heart. And continue on.

8.

Intention

The Motive

At the age of forty-three, when any other football player his age would have limped into retirement to play bad golf with a steadily thickening middle, Tom Brady instead sought a second wind by leaving the only team he had ever played for, the New England Patriots, for the Tampa Bay Buccaneers. It was a potentially cringe-worthy move that could have made him look like an overripe diva clinging to the spotlight too long. That spring, in May of 2020, he took part in a charity golf exhibition match in Florida with Phil Mickelson, Tiger Woods, and Peyton Manning. It was a meaningless affair on a balmy, palm-waving day in the middle of the off-season. Yet a couple of hours before the event, broadcaster Charles Barkley spotted Brady running sprints in the parking lot of the golf club, pouring sweat in the tropical heat.

"What the hell are you doing?" Barkley said incredulously.

"I'm trying to win a Super Bowl," Brady said.[1]

When the most prominent figure at the very top of an organization is the most intentional person in it, the impact is pervasive. Intention is more than just a declarative statement of temporary purpose. It's the conscious decision to work toward a self-crafted identity, to refuse to let events—or other people—decide who and what you will be.

Without intentionality, how else could Brady have overcome the following draft evaluation to become the greatest quarterback in league annals? "Poor build," a scout wrote of him back in 2000. "Skinny, lacks great physical stature and arm strength, lacks mobility and the ability to avoid the rush, lacks a really strong arm." The report went on: "Can't drive the ball down the field. Does not throw a really tight spiral, system-type player who can get exposed if forced to ad-lib. Gets knocked down easily."[2]

The draft evaluation would in time become infamous, one of those historical misjudgments on a par with a talent scout's assessment of Fred Astaire's screen test: "Can't act; slightly bald; can dance a little."

"Poor build . . . Gets knocked down easily." What if Brady had accepted that as the final judgment, surrendered to the opinion that it defined who he was, and ever would be? Over years of writing about Brady for the *Washington Post*, what became clear was the extent of his self-creation. The draft evaluation wasn't deliberately insulting. It was, at the time, indisputable. "I wasn't born a prodigy," Brady acknowledged in the spring of 2021. He was not a natural mover; he had the slow, flat gait of a platypus. As a thrower he lacked the arm of more gifted quarterbacks. Physically, he had long, attenuated, endomorphic limbs that indeed appeared somewhat toneless. Was the draft evaluation so inaccurate? No, it wasn't. It was merely the truth—but the incomplete truth.[3]

As Richard Branson has written, "Intention in its very essence is a futuristic act."[4]

Brady would go on to prove that any kid with perfectly ordinary athletic prospects, a middle-of-the-packer, could construct greatness. At every stage from childhood on Brady intentionally cured physical shortcomings, overcoming external skepticism about his abilities with study and sweat. His main driver, he once told me for a *Washington Post* profile, was "insecurity."[5]

As a freshman in high school at Junipero Serra in California, he was a clumsy-footed benchwarmer on a 0-8 team that failed to score a single touchdown. "I didn't even know how to put pads in my pants," he has said.[6]

From then on, it was one act of desperate self-improvement after another. He attended youth football summer camps at the nearby College of San Mateo, run by a renowned coach named Tom Martinez, who was such a stickler for mechanics that he would position boys in front of a brick wall and tell them to make a throwing motion, and then examine the scrapes on their knuckles. With the correct overhand silhouette, the knuckles would be clean, but a flawed motion would result in raked knuckles and scabs. Martinez insisted every time Brady threw something, anything, it should be intentional, aimed at a target. Even a wad of paper at a trash can.[7]

But those feet. Those feet required even more work. Brady's high school coach, Tom MacKenzie, told Brady he had a good upper body, but "the lower body of a scrub." The remark chafed, and so did jokes from his teammates about his duck-like gait. The team was required to do a "five-dot" agility drill, in which players jabbed their feet in a staccato tempo at a series of marked spots.

Brady didn't just do it at team practice. He spray-painted five dots on the floor of the family garage. He did the drill every single morning before school.

He spent four years at the University of Michigan fighting his way off the bench. He started out seventh on the depth chart. His turn at practice always seemed to come last, with the third-string linemen when the squad faced long yardage. He bristled with defensiveness and complained to head coach Lloyd Carr about his practice time compared to other quarterbacks. "I just don't feel like I'm getting my shot," Brady said. An unsympathetic Carr told him, "Worry about yourself. Quit worrying about what other people are doing." Brady was prone to sulk about it, until, in one of the most important pivots in his career, he saw a university sports psychologist named Greg Harden. When Brady lamented that he only seemed to get on the field when it was third down with eight yards to go, Harden replied, "What's wrong with that? If you can do it when it's third and eight, then everyone will know you can do it on third and four." It was a piece of advice Brady never forgot.

"You can look at it one way, and never get a bit better," Brady reflected years later. "Or you can put it on yourself to get better."[8]

Even as a senior Brady had to split time with a sophomore, Drew Henson, whom coaches saw as more talented. But Brady took responsibility for himself, refused to blame others, and finally seized the starting job all for himself. In the final game of his college career he led the team to a thrilling come-from-behind victory over Alabama in the Orange Bowl, twice overcoming fourteen-point deficits. "It's really a shift in the mind," Brady later told filmmaker Gotham Chopra for the 2022 documentary series *Man in the Arena*. "You go from being a victim to being empowered by the fact that you went through something difficult, and you learned from it."

The cycle repeated itself. His physical performance at the annual NFL Combine, an event to evaluate potential draft picks, was unremarkable: he ran a slogging time of 5.28 seconds in the forty-yard dash. Nobody saw much in him. On draft night, he sat for hours as team after team passed on him, until his eyes welled up with tears. When he was finally drafted in the sixth round, with the 199th pick by the Patriots, he was again dead last on a depth chart.

But soon the team's general manager, Scott Pioli, started getting phone calls from security guards in the middle of the night, saying that some kid was trying to get into the facility. Pioli decided to drive over and check, and there was Brady's car in the lot at 1:00 a.m. Brady was inside, doing more film study.[9]

The work paid off. In September of Brady's second season with the team, the Patriots lost their $30 million star quarterback, Drew Bledsoe, to a chest injury. Coach Bill Belichick stunned the league by turning to the lowly sixth-round pick, Brady. It looked like an act of desperation, but Belichick knew better. "I don't think I'm going to be standing here in ten weeks talking about all of Tom Brady's mistakes," Belichick said. The rest is lore: young Brady led them to the playoffs with an 11-5 record and upset the favored St. Louis Rams in the Super Bowl. Suddenly Brady was no longer the awkward, grating striver, but the most envied young man in America, an NFL star, and a cover boy on the front of magazines.

Then, for the first time in his life, he lost his intention.

The trouble with stardom is that Donald Trump starts calling you. Pretty soon, if you're not careful, you become a guy with more invitations than accomplishments. After that first Super Bowl victory, Brady accepted every appearance and endorsement; he did beauty pageants and ads for car dealers. The next season the Patriots went just 9-7 and Brady had a case of exhaustion from trying to make strangers happy. The convenience store where he stopped every morning for his orange juice had turned "into a Sharpie party," he said. He would sign autographs for huge throngs, and when he tried to get away he heard someone say, "What a jerk." It was demoralizing.

After his second Super Bowl victory, he went to Europe. Alone.

He spent a week in London by himself going to museums. He went on to Paris, Florence, and Rome and sat in sidewalk cafés being another American twentysomething in black jeans sipping coffee and gazing at church spires. He was anonymous, and it recharged him. Brady came to a conclusion: His favorite hangout wasn't a nightclub or a celebrity fashion show, or a restaurant that served crème brûlée. It was the locker room.

He loved the plebeian surroundings, the no-frills atmosphere, with everyone in the same egalitarian gray sweats all working intently toward the same goal, and the explosive joy of the place when they won. He loved mastering the playbook, which was so thick "you would think we were building rockets," he said.[10] He loved the bonds with like-minded teammates, who were all so hypercompetitive that their time-killing games of backgammon became board-slamming battles, uproarious to the point that everyone in the building would crowd around to watch and you couldn't get a seat. Apart from his family life, his most real and intense emotions all happened in that locker room. It was a place where there were no extravagances, where no reward was given but could only be *earned*.[11]

This simple piece of self-understanding would impel Brady going forward. It simplified all his decisions. He realized that if he didn't marshal his physical and mental energies better, other people would use him up. He began to turn down seven-figure endorsement deals, unwilling to make the time commitment they required.

He became more preemptive and intentional about his body, realizing that the NFL's expedient needle-pill-knife medical culture had a tendency to ruin young men prematurely. Brady was accustomed to living with pain in his throwing elbow from bouts of tendinitis and in his legs from training with heavy weights. But after a consult with an alternative medicine practitioner and physical therapist named Alex Guerrero, who had a reputation for easing the pains of NFL players with an array of offbeat methods that emphasized muscle "pliability," Brady was shocked by how supple and pain-free he felt.[12]

When he tore knee ligaments in 2008 and developed a post-surgery staph infection that cost him an entire season, Brady got a preview of his life after football as an arthritic old man, and he didn't like it. He and Guerrero embarked on a wholesale program of change, fashioning a new training method with resistance bands, yoga, alternative therapies, floods of hydration, and a strict anti-inflammatory diet. He quit sugars, white flour, processed foods. The result was a more tensile athlete who suddenly felt he might have years ahead of him.[13]

A routine that had begun with three visits to Guerrero a week became a codified, all-encompassing, seven-day-a-week lifestyle. Brady had always been scrupulous in his habits, but now he paid attention to the effects of the smallest things on his energy and performance. He calculated everything he did according to just two columns: there were "inputs" or "outputs."[14]

As Brady's intentionality grew and the Super Bowl tallies mounted, he began to talk openly about playing into his mid-forties. There was just one problem: not everyone on the New England Patriots had the same intentions that Brady did.

Conventional NFL wisdom, and some sketchy numerical analysis, said that a quarterback couldn't continue to play to the age of forty without "falling off a cliff" statistically. In fact, there was no hard evidence for such a thing. But to Brady's frustration, stereotypes of aging began to color perceptions of his play. They were more persuasive to some people than his actual performance. Head coach Bill Belichick believed, as a policy, in releasing veterans sooner rather than later and freshening his roster with youth, and he refused to commit to Brady with a new long-term contract extension. It touched an old sore spot, reawoke the underestimated grinder who was drafted too low. Brady was tired of cold Boston winters and Belichick's withholdingness. He craved a fresh start—and to prove that he could expand the age envelope and win another big one.

Tampa Bay, with its tourmaline waters, offered a completely different venue for all of that. As rigid and controlled as the New England Patriots were, that's how freewheeling the Tampa Bay Buccaneers were under their coach Bruce Arians, who drank beer with his players and called plays with a wide-open philosophy he styled as "no risk it, no biscuit."[15]

Brady didn't burst into the Tampa locker room braying his intention to win a Super Bowl. He never said, "I'm going to teach you how to win the big one." But they all heard about him doing those sprints in the golf course parking lot. The first thing he did when he arrived in Tampa was to muster receivers to run routes in the dead of summer at a high school practice field. He organized meetings with his offensive teammates, independent of the coaches, to help him learn the playbook.

Later, Brady reflected, "They're only going to trust and respect you if they see you do the work first. And if you're not willing to do it, then why should they be willing to do it?"[16]

His six Super Bowl rings gave him silent credibility, but it was his daily intentionality that was more important in fully seeding their belief. What he brought to the Bucs culture was the example that "the little things mattered," Arians asserted.[17] Most NFL teams do things right about 95 percent of the time. That's pretty good—unless you're trying to build a bridge, in which case 95 percent gets you a bridge that collapses. Brady gave the Bucs the 100 percent, the uncut corner, the last bit of applied workload required to get to a Super Bowl.

What Brady did was show the Bucs *why he wins*," running back Leonard Fournette observed. His personal mania bled over into other units, including the defense, which he would coolly prey on in practice if he saw an opening. Brady was renowned around the league for paying practice squad players if they intercepted him. It was their job to imitate the opposition. Some quarterbacks resented it when they were intercepted in practice. Paying for it was Brady's way of saying he appreciated the exposure because it prevented a larger one on game day.[18] Defensive coordinator Todd Bowles noticed his own players sharpening their techniques in response.

"They saw how hard he works at everything and how diligently he does it," Bowles said. ". . . You don't want to be embarrassed at practice by Brady picking on you, so you better pick your game up."[19]

Brady's intentionality had a measurable effect on the Buccaneers. Before Brady's arrival the Buccaneers had led the league in penalties in 2019. But now they became as tightly tucked in as a shirttail and wiped out two-thirds of those penalty flags. It meant one hundred yards' worth of improvement, the length of an entire football field. In a late pivotal win against Green Bay, they had not a single penalty.

They had also been the most turnover-prone team in the NFL in 2019, yielding thirty interceptions and eleven fumbles. But with Brady, the Bucs flipped the numbers. He gave up just twelve interceptions, while their defense forced twenty-five turnovers from opponents, a differential that was fifth best in the league.

Broadcast analyst Michael Irvin, a former three-time Super Bowl champion with the Dallas Cowboys, summarized Brady's full impact on the Buccaneers. "Greatness doesn't matter if you can't get everyone around you to be great," Irvin said. "If you can't get all those other guys to play with you, all you got is talent, and you won't win anything. There is physical talent, but then there is the talent to control and manage and work with the people around you." And that's what Brady brought.[20]

By the playoffs, Brady's intentionality was monstrous. They became the first NFL team ever to score thirty points per game in the postseason, and when they beat Green Bay by 31–26 in the NFC Championship Game to reach the Super Bowl, Brady made it clear he had no intention of settling for anything less than a title. He came into the locker room to find some of his teammates weeping for joy—most of them had never even *been* to a Super Bowl. "What the fuck are you crying for?" Brady growled furiously. "We're not done yet!" Players surreptitiously wiped away their tears.[21]

By then, Brady could have demanded anything of them, they so believed in him. His teammate LeSean "Shady" McCoy told commentator Pat McAfee, "He could say to me, 'Shady, go walk on that water; you won't drown.' I'm going to be like, 'Okay.'"[22]

The Super Bowl final score, as the record shows, was a 31–9 rout over Kansas City. Brady threw for three touchdowns, and only eight of his passes fell incomplete all night. It was quite simply "our best game of the year," Brady said afterwards.

Winning a Super Bowl was hardly a one-man feat. "I can't play defense; I can't tackle; I can't catch; I can't run with it," Brady pointed out later.[23] And yet. Without question, Brady's individual intention had mattered greatly.

"I think we knew this was going to happen, didn't we?" he said slyly after the game.[24]

Of course, for all the rewards, Brady's intentionality carries a price, too. His professional focus means he leads a fairly blindered and circumscribed life. He laughingly revealed after the Super Bowl victory that his then-wife, Gisele Bündchen, who is from Brazil, taught their three children a Portuguese phrase that translates as "Daddy doesn't know anything."[25]

But it's not always a laughing matter. His relentless focus blinded him to the fact that he was neglectful of their home life, prompting a confrontation, he admitted in a Howard Stern interview. "Her point was, 'Of course this works for you . . . but it doesn't work for me,'" he told Stern. "I had to check myself."[26] Brady has conceded, "Everything comes at a cost. . . . If you want to focus on one aspect of your job then other things are going to fail."[27]

One cost of Brady's intentionality was an eventual divorce. Another was that he acquired a reputation for ruthlessness. In 2022, he abruptly announced his retirement, though he had a year remaining on his Tampa contract. "I am not going to make that competitive commitment anymore," he said in a fey purported farewell announcement. Note the choice inherent in that statement. He didn't say he couldn't do it anymore, merely that he wouldn't.

Brady unretired just six weeks later, provoking speculation that his sabbatical had merely been a power play. The *Boston Globe* reported he had tried to engineer a contractual extrication and move to the Miami Dolphins, partly in exchange for some franchise control and only returned to Tampa when it fell through. If true, such conduct might seem offensive to naïve fans who believe that NFL franchises are deserving of loyalty. In fact, NFL teams are cold business entities in which even the most beloved players are ultimately treated as disposable commodities and highly manipulative owners are loyal only to the bottom line. Brady, in seeking to maximize his value, options, and control, is no different from any other league power broker, unusual only in that he still wore a helmet and not a suit.[28]

Regardless of the motive, Brady's unretirement was just one more act of self-determination. With it he made clear that when he walked away it would be a purely intentional move.

No athlete has ever given a greater demonstration of how to use himself instead of being used up. Among other legacies he will leave, Brady is the healthiest great champion the NFL ever had, because of his revolutionary decision to reject Mesozoic training methods and chart his own course with his long-term health. Large numbers of his teammates not only followed him on the field but also followed his training program. He has significantly altered ideas of competitive fitness, recovery, and longevity. And even as he turned forty-five, he still appeared to have plenty of life left in that supple arm.

At some point, Brady will eventually become just another unsuave, plodding person, who diminishes like the rest of us. But when he takes that long, slow walk back toward averageness, remember this about him: Had Brady listened to conventional wisdom, had he accepted the judgments of others, he might never have won a thing. His greatness was not in the power of his arm but in the power of his intention to decide for himself who he wanted to be.[29]

It's not enough for a leader to simply have strong intentions. Others have to perceive you as having *good* intentions. Anyone who aspires to lead should ask him- or herself, *What is your intent toward others? What exactly do you want from and for them?* If the sole answer is *a boost to my career*, then chances are that you belong on the bottom rung of an organization rather than at the top.

"If you don't care about the people you work with, you're hosed," Brady remarked shortly after winning his seventh Super Bowl. "And you better get out of that leadership role. Or you better find a way to become more caring and empathetic to the people you're working with. People want to do their best. And you've got to give them tools to be their best. . . . You've got to motivate *everybody*. . . . And it obviously starts at the top. And everybody is going to look at the leader and say, is this the person I want to follow?"[30]

The social psychologist Robert Hogan, a pioneer in using personality assessment to profile leaders, contends that we study leadership from exactly the wrong perspective. We tend to evaluate it—poorly—by looking at individuals who aggressively get to the top. When, in fact, we should evaluate potential leaders by asking those below them whether they find them worth working for. "The academic study of leadership has failed, and the reason is that it focuses on the leader when the appropriate focus is on the followers," Hogan has observed. "The focus should be on the workforce or the team, and what they perceive. Because if they don't perceive the right thing, you're through."[31]

People have to grant their cooperation for any idea to work, no matter how brilliant you are. And if they distrust your intentions, if they find you selfish or not genuine, they will withhold it. In an office setting, staff will get alienated and quit working as hard, and pretty soon the organization will enter a death spiral of "high turnover, high absenteeism, low productivity, and low customer satisfaction ratings," Hogan observes.

Hogan therefore identifies good intentions as the most essential quality in any leader. "Credibility as a leader depends vitally on perceived integrity: keeping one's word, fulfilling one's promises, not playing favorites, and not taking advantage of one's situation."[32]

Pat Summitt once sharply articulated, "People don't care how much you know until they know how much you care." Studies by the eminent neuropsychologist and Princeton professor Susan T. Fiske support this contention. Knowledge is actually the *second* quality that followers look for in a leader, according to Fiske; long before anyone assesses your expertise, they will neurocognitively assess your intentions and whether your motives toward them are warm or cold. Once they determine your intent, only *then* do they "decide whether the other is competent to enact those intents," Fiske observes.[33]

A pair of managerial assessment experts, Jack Zenger and Joseph Folkman, set out to study the question of whether it's particularly necessary for a leader to be liked. They surveyed impressions of 51,836 executives and found that just 27 who ranked in the bottom quartile of likability were rated highly as leaders by their subordinates. In other words, "the chances that a manager who is strongly disliked will be considered a good leader are only about one in 2000," they wrote.[34]

We've all met the type in offices: the world is full of executives with ill intentions, climbers who scrabble over others and impose their will on underlings. They use people to get to the top and, once there, imagine that leadership is about personal perks and commanding others to do their bidding. That's not leadership. It's warlording.

And it misapprehends the nature of real authority. The fact is, a team can destroy any leader.

Why is it so often the case that an organization led by a seemingly strong personality implodes, while a less assuming character succeeds? Because so many organizations make the same continual misjudgment they have made since *Mutiny on the Bounty*: they mistake the autocratic voice for a leaderly one and dominance for decision-making. Making true collaboration rare, and workplaces miserable.[35]

During the 2021 season, a coach named Urban Meyer experienced a modern-day mutiny at the head of the Jacksonville Jaguars, and became one of the most infamous busts in NFL history. Meyer was a high-profile hire from the college ranks, where he could push around scholarship-dependent boys. But at the pro level he was found out. Staff fragged him with a series of press leaks. Among the allegations that made their way public: that Meyer called his fellow coaches losers (though he had personally hired them) and his players "dipshits." He kept short hours while demanding exhaustive efforts from others, and on one occasion famously didn't bother to fly home with his team after a loss, and was instead captured on social media grinding in a bar. He lasted just thirteen games. The Jaguars were 2-11 when he was fired.[36]

Meyer failed to realize what every leader should: "Before people decide what they think of your message, they decide what they think of *you*," a team of social psychologists observed in the *Harvard Business Review*.[37]

The renowned anthropologist Christopher Boehm has a term for what a team does to an intolerable leader: it's called a "leveling mechanism." Boehm, the former director of the Jane Goodall Research Center at the University of Southern California, describes eloquently in essays such as "Political Primates" the ways in which followers are, subtly, the real rulers of hierarchies.

Pyramid-shaped organizations tend to be constructs of our own making. According to Boehm, we created them early in human history, not to elevate tyrants but for the sake of working efficiently in groups: someone had to organize the hunt. In these ancient human societies, intention of the leader mattered enormously. Those who sought to get a selfish edge or more than their fair share, or who acted as "self-aggrandizing political upstarts," were taken care of swiftly and brutally with leveling mechanisms that included ostracism, shaming, ejection, and even killing. "In effect these egalitarian bands did something very special about the problem of power," Boehm writes. "They arrived at a largely implicit 'social contract,' by which each political actor conceded his personal pursuit of dominance." Leveling mechanisms are as original to us as fire, Boehm suggests.[38]

Leveling mechanisms still exist, if in subtler form, as Urban Meyer learned. NBA championship coach Pat Riley, now the president of the Miami Heat basketball team, once described how the leveling dynamic can ruin an organization. "This is what happens whenever people on a team decide not to trust," Riley has observed. "Everyone will gear down their effort until they're doing just enough to get by. They want, subconsciously, to enroll everyone else in their cycle of disappointment."[39]

In the same week that Meyer was fired, a fascinating contrast played out with the Baltimore Ravens and their longtime coach, John Harbaugh. In the closing minutes of a game with the Green Bay Packers, the Ravens scored a touchdown to trail by the agonizingly close margin of just one point. Harbaugh faced a crucial call. He gathered his team on the sideline, and a microphone picked up the conversation. Leadership can be hard to capture, but you know it when you hear it, and you heard it from Harbaugh. Here's the thing: Harbaugh didn't issue orders to his players. He asked them what *they* intended to do.

"We want to kick it or go for it?" he asked. "What do you all think?"

Did they want to play it safe, and kick the extra point for the tie? Or should they play for the win, and go for the riskier two-point play?

"What do you want?" he asked again. "What does everybody want . . . Want to try for it?"

"Go for two," his quarterback, Tyler Huntley, said. "Let's win, Coach."

"All right," Harbaugh said. "Let's try it."

So, they tried it—and the play failed. They lost by a point. Harbaugh then stood up in the postgame press conference and shouldered all the blame for the call, refusing to deflect blame on his players.

In return, the Ravens full-throatedly supported him. "Anyone who second-guesses that is wrong," tight end Mark Andrews declared. The Ravens fought hard for Harbaugh to the end of the season to remain in viable playoff contention, even as they struggled with injuries to nine key players, including their star quarterback Lamar Jackson. Rarely has a team exhibited such cohesion under tough circumstances as the Ravens did for Harbaugh in 2021.[40]

The source of true power is not individual authority. The source of true power is buy-in.

The very best leaders don't tell people what to do. They ask them what they want to do together. They recognize that all anybody really wants from a leader, whether elite NFLers or laborers at their desks, is someone who works well with others in the room, who has expertise certainly, but who puts the enterprise first and creates the conditions for success.

Hogan and his colleagues Robert B. Kaiser and S. Bartholomew Craig observe in their organizational study titled "Leadership and the Fate of Organizations" that no individual leader, no matter how strong, is directly responsible for results. There are simply too many factors involved in a complicated enterprise. What great leaders do is establish the context in which all others perform. They don't determine or guide an outcome alone, they *enable* it.[41]

All great leaders thus have a fundamental sense of their reliance on others, and an underlying modesty about their role, even those with powerful personalities. Summitt once turned to her assistant coaches on the bench and said urgently, "Help me to help them." It's not a bad trait to look for, in trying to assess whether someone should be granted authority.[42]

Has there been a more effective modern corporate leader, with less jaw thrust, than Bob Iger of Disney? Initially, when Iger was named CEO in 2005, he seemed an unspectacular choice after years of steady service in the company. A "loyal drone," one critic labeled him. A key shareholder insisted "there are stronger candidates out there." Iger's predecessor Michael Eisner damned him with faint praise as "not brilliantly creative." So how did he become one of the most influential and transformative leaders in the entertainment industry? "The answer . . . lies in his discipline, his thoughtful and straightforward management style and a knack for forging trust with business partners," the *Los Angeles Times* wrote. Iger's chief philosophy as the company steward, he says, was to lead in a way that was "not political in nature, that is hospitable."[43]

So many businesses—especially sports teams—mistake hospitable leadership as somehow weak. Yet it's a noticeable fact that the longest-tenured and most successful coaches in the NFL are not the spit screamers. Andy Reid of the Kansas City Chiefs almost never raises his voice. Mike Tomlin of the Pittsburgh Steelers, Pete Carroll of the Seattle Seahawks, and even Bill Belichick of the Patriots all share an interesting self-effacement and marked knack for creating loyal staff.

It's continually startling to top leaders in the military how often corporate executives and coaches imitate martial attitudes, without seeming to understand that it's the self-effacing leaders who really forge great outfits. Rob Lively, who retired after twenty-eight years with the Army Special Operations Command at Fort Bragg to form a strategic consultancy, has observed that for all that tactical experience matters, the most essential element of any successful unit is "brotherhood." Lively remarked to The Cipher Brief, a digital platform that connects the private sector with security experts: "You serve with passion and intensity, because you don't want to let your brothers down, whether it's obtaining a resource for them to do their job or fighting beside them. I'm surprised that a lot of these companies don't understand that."[44]

Perhaps no American subculture has been as subject to the warlord misinterpretation as football. It's a game of brutal collisions, and for over one hundred years it has bred coaches with dictatorial traits. But that has changed significantly in the last couple of decades, largely thanks to the influence of one man, Tony

Dungy, who from 1996 until his retirement in 2008 intentionally set out to prove that a gentler leadership template could work in the game. He was inducted into the Hall of Fame in 2016, and his enshrinement biography begins with this quote from him: "The secret to success is leadership and good leadership is all about making the lives of your team members or workers better."[45]

Dungy's basic coaching philosophy was shaped by his father, Wilbur, a professor and a military veteran who served with the famed Tuskegee Airmen, and who gave his son a lesson in self-governance that he never forgot. Dungy was thirteen years old when he watched the 1968 Olympics on television and saw USA track medalists Tommie Smith and John Carlos bow their heads and raise black-gloved fists on the podium in Mexico City. Coming shortly after the assassination of Dr. Martin Luther King Jr., the protest alternately electrified and infuriated Americans, and public debate raged about the value of the gesture. Dungy asked his father whether Smith and Carlos had been right to protest, and whether he should join in race demonstrations.

Dungy expected Wilbur, a proud vet, to give him a yes or no answer. He half expected Wilbur to say, "You should always stand at attention during the anthem." Instead, Wilbur began to ask him a series of questions.

"What do you think?" Wilbur asked. "Is it helping the situation?" Tony didn't know if protests and demonstrations were helping or not; he only knew that everyone seemed to be joining in them. "If you think it's making things better, then do it," Wilbur replied. "But don't do it because everyone else is."[46]

Sometimes the quietest man in the room was the most powerful, Dungy learned from Wilbur. His father had come out of the air force to earn a doctorate in biology from Michigan State and was the first black professor at Jackson College, where he taught life sciences. But Wilbur was reticent about his accomplishments; he almost never talked about them—so reticent that Dungy didn't know his father had flown with the famed Tuskegee unit until he died. Wilbur taught that you set high standards, didn't complain aloud about obstacles, and that your inner integrity mattered more than any outside opinion. "Dad, you knew the answer to that; why didn't you tell 'em?" Dungy would say. Wilbur just replied, "I like to listen. I like to take in information."

All of it informed Dungy's own "Quiet Strength" style as a leader, with which he transformed two longtime losing franchises, the Tampa Bay Buccaneers and the Indianapolis Colts, into perennial contenders. What he eventually became proudest of, even more than his achievement as the first black head coach to win a Super Bowl, was his reputation as a benevolent winner who treated his players with supreme dignity. Dungy was by no means easy to play for. "No excuses, no explanations" was his mantra. Yet he combined demandingness with plain decency, and explicitly told his colleagues and players that his aim was to pair the words "champion" and "good guy" in the same sentence.[47]

"His coaching philosophy and coaching methods, his leadership style, was that he treated you so well, he treated you like such a professional, like a grown-up, that you just didn't want to let him down," Peyton Manning reflected years later. "I mean, that's how I felt, and how just about all the players felt. They didn't want to disappoint him, so they played harder for him. They wanted to make that great catch for him or great tackle for him because of the way he treated you. Look, there's different ways to motivate players, so there's scare tactics, where if you make a mistake, you're gonna lose your job and get cut, and that can make a lot of players play harder and stay on their toes. But Dungy's was different."[48]

It took immense patience for Dungy to win a head coaching job at all, a fifteen-year wait that he somehow accepted charitably. At the end of his playing career in 1981 with the Pittsburgh Steelers his head coach, Chuck Noll, made him the youngest assistant coach in league history, at the age of twenty-five. There were just ten black assistant coaches in the entire league at the time. It would be 1996 before Tampa Bay hired Dungy as a head coach and gave him the headset. It wasn't just that he was a black man. He also knew it was because he didn't fit the classic mold of a yeller. People saw his personality as too mild, and just didn't believe it would work to coach football that way. As one magazine writer noted in a piece on Dungy's against-the-grain quietude, "the heyday of coach as emotionally intimidating bastard is not done." The headline on the story asked, "Can This Nice Guy Finish First?"[49]

When Dungy finally got his chance, it was with the worst team in the league. The Buccaneers had suffered twelve seasons of double-digit losses in thirteen years. But Dungy took them to the playoffs in just his second year at their helm, and he did it without shouting at anyone, or driving them. Coaches were traditionally expected to flaunt their obsessive work habits, to show off how early they got to the office and how many hours they put in on film study during an eighteen-hour day. But Dungy declared that office time didn't dictate success, working "efficiently" did, and insisted his coaches keep sane hours and have meals with their families. He tried to get home for dinner every night himself, and when he went to office in the dark before sunrise his wife, Lauren, would bring the kids by to have breakfast at the team facility before school.[50]

It was a traditional NFL method to fine players for petty offenses, like being late to meetings or violating dress codes. Dungy didn't see much use in that. He found it infantilizing. He would tell his players, "I'm not big on fines. I'm not big on any of that." What he did say to them was this: "If you're not on time it tells me one of two things. Either what we're doing in this room is not that important to you. Or it *is* important to you, but I can't depend on you." He never had much of a problem with guys being late.[51]

In Dungy's opinion, people didn't do what was asked of them because they thought they might get fined. They did what they were asked because they wanted to be part of something good.[52]

"He was very selective about who he was bringing into the locker room and to the team," Manning recalled. "The super selfish guys and the guys that weren't gonna buy into the team, they weren't getting into the building."[53]

Dungy betrayed his truest intentions on just one important occasion—and it cost him. Initially when he became Tampa's head coach, owner Malcolm Glazer and general manager Rich McKay assured him he had time to build a team the right way. But at the end of the 2000 season, the Buccaneers got to the doorstep of the Super Bowl only to lose in a painfully low-scoring NFC championship game to the St. Louis Rams, 11-6. Management suddenly became impatient. They leaned on Dungy to make a move he didn't believe in.

Blame for the loss fell, unfairly, on Dungy's young offensive coordinator, thirty-four-year-old Mike Shula. Dungy knew the Buccaneers' problems weren't Shula's fault. Their starting quarterback, Trent Dilfer, had gotten hurt and so had most of the offensive line. In fact, "Mike did exactly what I wanted him to do," Dungy recalled. "But our ownership, in their mind, was thinking, 'Gosh, we throw one touchdown we're in the Super Bowl.'" The men upstairs in the owner's suite wanted Dungy to fire Shula. Dungy wrestled with the decision: Did he do an injustice to Shula, or should he refuse to fire him, and lose his own job by alienating his bosses?[54]

Shula heard whispers of Dungy's predicament and rescued him. He offered to resign. Better for him to step down, Shula told Dungy, than for management to fire the entire staff. "If they let you go, then a lot of people lose their jobs," Shula said generously. Dungy agreed and accepted the resignation.

Almost immediately, Dungy knew it was a terrible mistake. "It wasn't the right thing and I didn't feel good about it," he recalled. It left the entire staff wounded, and they never recovered their cohesion. When the Bucs lost to the Philadelphia Eagles one year later in the 2001 wild card playoff round, Dungy and his staff got fired anyway.

Dungy rebounded by landing with the Indianapolis Colts, where he had the most promising young quarterback in the game in Peyton Manning. Shula bounced back, too, winding up as a head coach at his alma mater, Alabama. But Dungy swore not to betray his inner voice again. "I was a young coach at the time and I'm trying to balance, okay, these are my bosses and this is what they want; I'm under their authority. . . . But that taught me one thing right there: that I was *never* going to make a decision from then on that I didn't agree with in terms of the direction of my organization," he says.[55]

Dungy arrived in Indianapolis in 2002 determined not to abandon his convictions again. His genuineness made an immediate impression on Manning, who experienced something like what behavioralist Susan Fiske has described: Here was a leader from whom you sensed pure intentions and warm motives. Who was firm in his statements, yet expressed them without ever raising his voice, or using a foul or demeaning word. Manning was inclined to trust him and listen to him.[56]

Manning found Dungy's soft-power approach to coaching "unique," and it happened to be exactly what he needed at the time. Manning was a strongheaded but uneven player who was not yet close to the ruthlessly efficient all-time great he would become. Though he was obviously one of the most potent young players in the game, he was also a league leader in interceptions; as a rookie he had set a single-season record for interceptions that still stands, with twenty-eight. His win-loss mark entering his fifth season as a pro was still an indeterminate 32-32—he had lost as many games as he had won. "It was like, who am I going to be?" Manning remembered.[57]

The record book reflects a major difference in who Manning was as a quarterback before he was coached by Dungy, and who he was after. The numbers are stark. Dungy provided a new set of intentions to a young player who, despite his gifts, was quietly burdened. Press critics continually suggested that Manning, a prodigy and top draft pick, was not living up to a contract worth $48 million. Asked once what he intended to do with his money, Manning replied, "Earn it." On Dungy's first day in the Indianapolis offices, Manning came by to say hello. "I *want* to be coached," Manning told him almost pleadingly. He brought to Dungy's office seven pages of notes on a yellow legal pad. "These are the things I want to get better at," he said. It was an interesting admission of vulnerability by Manning, and he likely would not have made it to a coach with a less teacherly demeanor. "He wants to be great, and he wants you to *tell* him how to be great," Dungy thought to himself.[58]

Still, in their first season together, Manning threw nineteen interceptions, third most by any quarterback in the entire NFL. Dungy treaded carefully. Before he could really help Manning, he had to understand what was going on in the head of an undeniably intelligent, heady player, the context in which Manning was operating.

Dungy began by asking questions. What was Manning's intention when he threw the ball—why did he throw it there? As Dungy listened to Manning's explanations, he realized the quarterback had a legitimate reason for every misdirected pass. They were mistakes of *commission*, not omission, and Manning took full responsibility for them. In fact, Manning took too much responsibility for everything. It turned out that Manning felt pressure to carry the team, to compensate for all of their other weaknesses, especially on defense—in Manning's third season the Colts had given up more points than any other NFL team—with big scoring throws. They would look at film, and Manning would say, "I did that because if we were going to win the game, we gotta go for it there, I've gotta throw a touchdown pass. It was third down, and I didn't want to punt."[59]

Manning hated to punt. If they punted, it might be six minutes before he got the ball back.

"He felt he *had* to make every throw," Dungy recalls. "Every tough throw, he could explain to me why he made it. He wasn't making *reckless* decisions. It was what he thought was right."[60]

Dungy somehow had to convince Manning to restrain his arm, get across to him that sometimes a better decision was a more discreet one. Throw a shorter ball and let a teammate try to make a play—or even throw the ball away.

A key facet of intentionality is patience. Patience was Dungy's most pronounced quality, and it was his gift to Manning as a quarterback. Under Dungy's steady tutelage, Manning began to see the virtue of watching and waiting for his openings, and accepting a Plan B. The coach appealed to Manning's intellect, framing the interceptions as a math problem. "Our offense is so good that if we get sixty-five plays in the game, we're going to do a certain amount of damage," Dungy told Manning. "But if we only get fifty plays, because we took needless chances and we gave the other team the ball a couple of extra times, that cuts down on fifteen chances we have to make something explosive happen."[61]

Dungy flipped the point of view and showed Manning how defenses were preying on his impatience. "They don't think you can be patient enough to throw the short pass, to throw it underneath," Dungy said. "They're *hoping* you're going to make that throw. You're doing exactly what they *want* you to do. You ought to take it as an insult."[62]

If Manning would discipline himself to make enough of the short, safe completions, it would cause the defense to lose their own patience and break down. Pick away at them, lull them. And when they overplayed and tried to blitz, blam. "*Now* you can burn 'em."

Patience wasn't complacent, Dungy taught. It was commanding.

Manning became a different creature. "Once he knew *why*," Dungy observes, "it was easy to get him to come on board." Over his next four seasons, Manning wouldn't yield more than ten interceptions. True to Dungy's word, now he could burn 'em. He lit the scoreboard at a record pace in 2004 with forty-nine touchdowns to just ten giveaways. In 2006, their Super Bowl season, he threw for thirty-one scores while being picked off by opponents just a career-low nine times. "I felt like my game really took another step once he got there, because of that insight," Manning says.[63]

The teasing, exploitative style Manning would show in his prime, baiting defenses with short precision passes only to blow them up deep, was born in those early sessions with Dungy. Ironically, a coach known for his pure intentions helped fashion a quarterback who was a master of deception. Manning would become ever better at toying with his intentions—underselling or overselling defenses, forcing them to continually guess where he was going—until by the end of his career he could fleece a defense just by flicking his eyes downfield. He kept opposing coaches awake at night. "We play number eighteen this week, no time to sleep," one said.[64]

Dungy would have a softer and more lasting personal impact on Manning, too. Manning's practice habits as he entered his prime were so obsessive that it led to a rare issue on which he disagreed with Dungy's philosophy. Manning would come out to the practice field Saturday mornings for what was supposed to be a last, light workout, and have cue cards full of plays in his hand that he wanted to run through like a final dress rehearsal. But Dungy declared Saturdays were "family days," unstructured affairs in which players could bring their children on the field. Manning would try to groove one last nuanced route with his receivers while children dodged around in the grass. He'd protest with annoyance to Dungy, "We don't have the concentration level we need here." He asked Dungy to banish the children. "Can't we leave the kids in the locker room?" Dungy refused. It drove Manning crazy.[65]

When Manning had kids, he finally understood. In 2011, Manning and his wife, Ashley, welcomed twins. In one of his last seasons, as a fade-armed veteran with the Denver Broncos, Manning went to head coach, John Fox, with a suggestion: Why didn't he institute "Family Days" when players could bring their children to the practice field? "The kids need to know where their fathers are," Manning said, echoing his former coach. The change of heart tickled Dungy, who never tired of telling the story of Manning, and was much prouder of that influence than of any strategy he imparted. [66]

Dungy would lose sight of his true intentions just once more in his career before he retired at the age of just fifty-three to better devote himself to his family and his faith. This time, it was more amusing than serious and had a happy outcome. In the 2007 Super Bowl XLI against the Chicago Bears, the Colts faced a player with searing speed in Devin Hester, who set an enduring NFL record for most kickoffs returned for touchdowns. Dungy, typically, decided that discretion was the best way to deal with a threat like Hester. For two weeks in the lead-up to the game, he had the Colts practice kicking the ball away from Hester. "We were going to kick it to the corners; we were going to squirt it, bounce it; we were not going to let him be a factor," Dungy remembered.

But the night before the game, Dungy attended a team chapel service and listened tensely as a preacher delivered a spirited sermon on David and Goliath. "David got the job done—he went right *at* that giant!" the preacher roared.

Dungy began to second-guess himself. *This is the Super Bowl— we can't play scared of Devin Hester*, he thought. They needed to go *at* him, like David went at the giant. By the next morning, Dungy had totally reversed the game plan for Hester. In his pregame speech to the Colts, first he addressed the weather. It was pouring outside, a rare Miami monsoon. "We're going to encounter a storm, and we will have to weather it," he warned them. Then he announced a new strategy on Hester. "We're gonna kick it *right* down the middle," he declared. "And when we pound him, they'll know we mean *business*, and that will set the tone. We will have taken away their best threat. And they will be *finished*."

The Colts kicked off, right at Devin Hester.

Twelve seconds later, Hester was in the end zone. He dodged, slipped two tacklers at once, cut hard inside and accelerated, breezed past pairs of outstretched hands, and was off and running free, untouched. It was a ninety-two-yard touchdown. And the Colts trailed 7–0.

On the sideline, Dungy just stood there thinking, *That is the dumbest thing I've ever done.* Rows of players stared at him, as if to say, "What were you thinking?"

Dungy said helplessly, "I told you we'd have a storm."

The Colts somehow regrouped, largely thanks to Dungy's forthrightness. "All you can do at that point is turn toward your team and say, 'You know what, that wasn't the right decision. But we've got to go forward; we can't look back now.'"

Dungy told his team, "You guys have to bail me out here." They did. They went on to win the game, 29–17, outscoring the Bears by 20 points over the final three quarters.[67]

Dungy would set the modern NFL record for consecutive play-off appearances with ten trips. Only twice in his thirteen-year career did his teams fail to make the postseason. He was the first NFL head coach to defeat all thirty-two teams in the league, and the only coach to amass six straight seasons of twelve wins or more. His regular season-winning percentage of .759 with the Colts would be higher than that of Vince Lombardi and Don Shula. But if you ask him what his real accomplishment was, he replies:

"*How* we did things was waaaaay more important than *what* we did."[68]

Epilogue

The Heart of Greatness

The elements we've explored—conditioning, practice, discipline, candor, culture, failure, and intention—these are at the root of acumen in any field, and they can give all of us, no matter our profession, the poised ability to think and choose more clearly. Still, these principles have to be activated by a deeper purpose. If you don't care about your chosen profession, you're just ditch digging. All the achievers in these pages have found meaning in their work that animates them.

Great athletes operate on more than sweat and method; their real fuel is aspiration. They're not just well-built machines. Their constitutions are systems, certainly, governed by physics and mechanics. Move an arm in a certain way enough times and it will improve its functionality. But that's not a complete explanation for their movement. For all that we know about physiology and neurology, something is left out. There's a blank in our understanding.

Somehow, athletes translate mere mechanics into phenomenal sensations and emotional experiences. A bird flies not solely because it's mechanically built to fly. It has motive—it seeks.

Great performers have motive. They embrace their craft with a wholehearted sense of exploration. This is what gives them real lift, the athletic jauntiness that makes excellence look nonchalantly beautiful.

You can see this adventurous love of craft in the face of the most intense pressures and excruciating losses. The greats aren't immune from deep trough seasons in which no amount of strategy can compensate for bad breaks. Steve Kerr and the Golden State Warriors had one of those in 2020, when they lost their two most important scorers, Steph Curry and Klay Thompson, to injuries. A young injury-strafed team went a league-worst 15-50. Kerr had to shift his aim from hunting a championship to one that any working person can relate to. It became an exercise in asking young players to show up every day for no immediate reward except self-respect and pride in craft, without "letting go of the rope," as he put it. Yet Kerr found himself thoroughly engaged. There was something so pure in the task of teaching young unheralded players with no expectations, that it turned out to be a welcome break from the pressure of trying to get a superstar-loaded group another trophy.[1]

"I enjoyed last season—when we had the worst record in the league—more than I enjoyed that last season when we went to the Finals," Kerr remarked when it was over. "We had young guys who were trying every day, working hard. We had a great energy, great spirit, great camaraderie. Losing sucked. But what you want is a good vibe. You want to look forward to going to the gym every day and seeing everybody."[2]

What gratified Kerr was that his culture of joy held: even in the losses they found ways to love the game, thanks to the atmosphere of free play he had instilled. As he told his player Andre Igoudala on the *Point Forward* podcast, "We still played music in practice, still made fun of each other, made fun of ourselves . . . And it mattered, especially when you're losing, that's when the culture has to matter . . . Here we were with the worst record in the league, but guys were enjoying the process of learning and growing and getting better . . . We must be doing something right." They were. In 2022, it would pay off with a fourth NBA Championship in eight years.

When people love their daily endeavor, they're the masters of themselves rather than prey to emotional turmoil and regret about what they're doing. That's important when circumstances seem overwhelming. As a dragon slayer of seventy-foot colossus swells, Laird Hamilton is more familiar with the overwhelming than anyone else on the planet. What helps him cope with those situations is that he's damn sure he wants to be there. Hamilton has seen too many dabblers who thought they wanted to catch a big wave when they really didn't. To slide down a water cliff and be chased by a white-salt avalanche, you better love the ocean.

"If you're there because it's what you want, what you believe in, if you're there for the pure reason, you will respond correctly," Hamilton says. "Then you'll be like, well, this is part of what happens, this is what you do, and so you're prepared to take the consequences. And if you're not, if you are there for any other reasons, then you'll wish you weren't, and you'll freak out and want to get out of there."[3]

Sometimes there *is no good choice*, and sometimes the competition is simply better. What carries the best performers in those instances? Their love of the endeavor for its own sake—what it calls up of their effort, how it tests the integrity of their own internal judgments, and their willingness to be actors rather than spectators.

The best call I ever saw Pat Summitt make came during one of her hardest seasons. In 2004, Pat experienced some second-guessing, and also self-doubt. She had won six national championships by then, but it had been several seasons since she had hung a banner in the rafters at the University of Tennessee, as Connecticut under Geno Auriemma ascended and became preeminent. One day, Pat opened her mailbox and withdrew an anonymous letter telling her that she was "past it" and needed to retire. She was just fifty-two.

That year, Pat had a team ranked No. 1, with potentially all the pieces to win another title. But halfway through the season, her starting point guard, Loree Moore, tore the anterior cruciate ligament in her knee. It was a sickening turn of events. Moore was their floor leader, a whip-armed passer, and their best defender. Her loss seemed almost sure to sink the season.

But Pat found a way to reconfigure the team and give it new heart.

In the locker room on the morning after the injury, she calmly wrote Moore's statistics on a large whiteboard. She then drew an empty box score. One by one, Pat asked each of the eight healthy players on the roster if they could find a way to add two more points, or one more rebound, or one more steal per game to their averages. What did they think they could give, no matter how small? Each time a player answered, Pat put a mark on the board. By the time she was done, eight kids had filled up the box score. They knew they could do it.

Pat converted her most experienced senior forward, Tasha Butts, into a point guard and on every bus trip sat by her side and delivered an accelerated tutorial in decisions with the ball. Somehow, that shorthanded, reconfigured Tennessee team with no true point guard clawed their way to the NCAA Final Four—though they twice had to sink last-second shots to get there. And I never saw Pat have more fun or love a team more.

In the national tournament semifinals in New Orleans, Tennessee met a favored Louisiana State squad that was playing in front of a tremendous home crowd. They fought to a stalemate. With six seconds left, the score was tied 50–50. But LSU had the ball.

Time-out. As the crowd rose roaring to its feet, there seemed just two possible outcomes. Either LSU would sink a shot for the win or the teams would go to overtime. And in overtime Pat's thin team, who were breathing heavily, would be doomed.

That's when Pat made the call. Maybe the greatest call I ever saw her make. In the huddle, she called a trap—two players would try to hem in the ballhandler. But this was not just any trap. It was a gambling, all-in, headlong, get-a-steal-or-go-home trap. Pat ordered her biggest players up the floor to collapse on the ball-handler. Which left the basket momentarily uncovered.

As soon as the ball was inbounded, Tennessee players sprinted to it—if LSU found an opening, it was an easy score.

But Tennessee swarmed. It was like trying to pass through a chain-link fence. Center Ashley Robinson flailed her arms—and swatted away the ball—and a forward named Shyra Ely pounced on it. Without even fractional hesitation Ely scooped the ball up and flung it across midcourt, to her streaking teammate LaToya Davis, who gathered it in and soared to the rim. Layup. Basket. Buzzer.

Game over. Final score Tennessee 52, LSU 50.

Pat had completely flipped the pressure, changed the entire dynamic, and orchestrated the winning shot.

Had Pat made the right call? If so, only because every one of her players had executed with discipline, been so conditioned and well practiced that they knew exactly where to go and what to do when the ball came free.

A few minutes later I found Pat in a back hallway. She was bent over with a hand to her chest. "I can't catch my breath," she said.

"I imagine not; that was a damn heart attack," I said.

"No, I'm not kidding," she said. "I'm having trouble breathing."

It turned out she was having heart arrhythmia, the first of a cascade of medical issues—no doubt some of them pressure induced—that would shorten her career and lead to her premature passing at just sixty-four. A day later Tennessee lost in the championship game to a UConn team that was simply too much and Pat went home to go on heart medication. But I'd never known her so proud of a team, or heedless of a defeat. And I never forgot the total, consuming pleasure with which she coached them, or the pure nerve.

Pat made that call by being highly deliberative; she sought input from her assistant coaches, and considered all the angles—and then she committed with her whole soul. And never regretted it. She had clarity about her values, understood what she could affect and what she could not, and had a wry self-deprecation, win or lose, that aided her in hard times. "I'm just a P.E. teacher," she liked to say. Consider: Though she won eight national titles, over a thirty-eight-year career, Summitt finished the season a loser thirty times. If she was only in it to win, she couldn't have lived with that. It wasn't the winning that sustained her; it was her pure love of the contest.

"You like pulling triggers, don't you?" I asked.

"Love it," she said. "*Love* it."

Pat's gone, but my fascination with the right call, and the realization that Pat didn't need to win it all to love her work—*love it*—lingers.

"Who can describe the athletic heart?" I hope these chapters have partly dismantled that mysterious mechanism, for closer examination. When you choose a profession for love, you find that last invisible measure, the one that can vault you into a more imaginative state than just digging a trench for pay. Those who find something they can fully immerse themselves in tend to discover that work acquires its own impetus. It becomes a natural part of what you do—you begin to live your work. And when that happens, you can't lose. Like Hamilton riding the energy and undercurrent of a wave, the most free-flowing performances occur.

Acknowledgments

There is one principle left out of these pages: luck. In any pursuit of success, you need some good luck. Luck is getting born the daughter of a writer and *inheriting* a great agent. For more than twenty-five years, Esther Newberg of ICM has provided opportunities for this inky, insecure junior scrounger. More than that, she's a dear family friend known simply as "Treasure."

Without Karyn Marcus of Gallery Books, there would be no legible pages between these covers. There would only be a cat in yarn, trying to frantically chew her way out of a tangle. Somehow, Karyn cut the book free, with her delicate pencil and considered judgment. She also patiently coaxed pages forward despite two years of Covid, multiple family crises, repeated missed deadlines, and one attempt to quit. She is simply the most generous and sure-guiding book editor I've ever worked with, for which she has not only my professional but my personal gratitude. Thanks also to Rebecca Strobel of Gallery for all the finishing touches.

Marty Jenkins, my beloved twin brother, for several years now has abetted other members of his family in publishing books as a stealth writer-researcher, fact-rescuer, and companionable sharer of insomnia and ideas. Without his steadying hand under the elbow, it would never have gotten done. "When you agree with a brother, no fortress is as strong as your common life."

Editors Matt Vita and Matt Rennie of the *Washington Post* give more than jobs to their people. They give us a home-place to be that feels like a combination of championship team clubhouse, beer garden, play den, and pilot ready room. They pile talent on top of talent, and rewards on top of rewards, and it's hard to believe that work could be so much fun, but it's real. Playing for their dynasty is the greatest privilege of any sportswriter's life.

This writer is only as good as her material. Peyton Manning, Steve Kerr, Tony Dungy, Laird Hamilton, Jill Ellis, Ron Rivera, Tommy Amaker, Muffet McGraw, Bob Bowman, Frank Reich, Kyle and Mike Shanahan, David Cutcliffe, Diana Nyad, Bonnie Stoll, Pia Nilsson, Lynn Marriott, Dana Cavalea, Tom House, Bob Iger, Mark Cuban, and Robert Hogan all graciously gave of their time, thoughts, and insights about that dazzling apparatus, the athletic heart.

Finally, nothing matters, nothing counts, nothing is worthwhile, nothing means anything without the beauteous Nicole Bengiveno.

Endnotes

PROLOGUE

1. Sally Jenkins, "7 Pete Sampras," *Sports Illustrated*, February 9, 1995, https://vault.si.com/vault/1995/02/09/7-pete-sampras.
2. Billie Jean King, author's personal conversation.
3. Pat Summitt, author's personal conversation.
4. Sally Jenkins, "Barkley Puts Fierce Move on the Game," *Washington Post*, March 23, 1988.
5. Author interview with Michael Phelps for the *Washington Post*, June 14, 2012.
6. Author interview with Chris Evert for the *Washington Post*, May 13, 2020.
7. Billie Jean King, author's personal conversation.
8. Dan Patrick, "Patrick Mahomes on the Dan Patrick Show," *The Dan Patrick Show*, January 28, 2021.
9. Sally Jenkins, "Football Is Changing. Bill Belichick Doesn't Think the Keys to Winning Ever Will.: In a Sport of Innovation, Longtime Patriots Coach Believes the Same Things That Have Made Him Successful Continue to Matter Most," WP Company LLC d/b/a *Washington Post*, September 25, 2018.
10. Sally Jenkins, "Natural Born Killer," *Sports Illustrated*, September 5, 1994, https://vault.si.com/vault/1994/09/05

/natural-born-killer-pete-sampras-seems-aloof-but-he-burns
-to-destroy-all-comers-on-the-court.

11. Sally Jenkins, "Agassi Is One Superstar with His Feet Planted Firmly on the Ground," *Washington Post*, August 30, 2000.

12. Sally Jenkins, "Love and Love He's Beaten His Demons, He's Won Over Brooke Shields. Could Andre Agassi Be All Grown Up?," *Sports Illustrated*, March 13, 1995, https://vault.si .com/vault/1995/03/13/love-and-love-hes-beaten-his -demons-hes-won-over-brooke-shields-could-andre-agassi -be-all-grown-up.

13. Ibid.

1. THE "RIGHT" CALL:
DECISIONS UNDER PRESSURE

1. Sally Jenkins, "Andy Reid Is Going for It," *Washington Post*, January 29, 2021.

2. Tom Brady Q&A, Adobe Summit 2020.

3. David Romer, "Do Firms Maximize? Evidence From the National Football League," *Journal of Political Economy* 114, no. 2 (April 2006).

4. Author interview with Michael J. Lopez, January 6, 2021 for the *Washington Post*.

5. Ibid.; Derrick Yam and Michael J. Lopez, "What Was Lost? A Causal Estimate of Fourth Down Behavior in the National Football League," *Journal of Sport Analytics*, June 24, 2019, 1–15; Michael J. Lopez, "Bigger Data, Better Questions, and a Return to Fourth Down Behavior," *Journal of Quantitative Analysis in Sports* 16, issue 2 (May 29, 2020): 73–79.

6. Lopez, "Bigger Data."

7. Chester I. Barnard, *The Functions of the Executive* (Cambridge: Harvard University Press, 1968), 193.

8. Author interview with David Cutcliffe, April 15, 2020.
9. Henry Mintzberg, Duru Raisinghani, and Andre Theoret, "The Structure of 'Unstructured' Decision Processes," *Administrative Science Quarterly* 21, no. 2 (June 1976): 246–75.
10. Ibid.
11. Ibid.
12. Author interview with Laird Hamilton, October 12, 2020.
13. Author interview with Tony Dungy, September 15, 2020.
14. Author interview with Laird Hamilton, October 12, 2020.
15. Author interview with Frank Reich, March 31, 2020.
16. Peter Limbach and Florian Sonnenberg, "Does CEO Fitness Matter?," CFR Working Paper No. 14-12 (rev3), University of Cologne, Center for Financial Research; Fernando Gomez-Pinilla and Charles Hillman, "The Influence of Exercise on Cognitive Abilities," *Comprehensive Physiology*, vol. 3, issue 1, January 2013, pp. 403–24, https://www .ncbi.nlm.nih.gov/pmc/articles/PMC3951958/.
17. Author interviews with Peyton Manning, April 18, 2022, and Tony Dungy, September 15, 2020.
18. Author interview with Peyton Manning, April 18, 2022.
19. Author interview with Frank Reich, March 31, 2020.
20. Jeff Bezos, Letter to Amazon shareholders, 2017. All Bezos letters to shareholders can be found at: https://ir.aboutamazon .com/annual-reports-proxies-and-shareholder-letters/default .aspx.
21. Sally Jenkins, "Racket Science," *Sports Illustrated*, April 29, 1991, https://vault.si.com/vault/1991/04/29/racket-science -billie-jean-king-has-been-a-dynamo-as-a-tennis-champion -promoter-television-commentator-businesswoman-and -feminist-but-she-may-be-even-more-compelling-in-her-latest -career-teaching.
22. Author interview with Pia Nilsson and Lynn Marriott, October 10, 2020.
23. Author interview with Peyton Manning, April 18, 2022.

24. Pete Carroll, *Flying Coach* podcast, theringer.com, June 3, 2020.
25. Author interview with Tommy Amaker, August 26, 2020.
26. Greg Sands, interview with Steve Young, "Life Is More Athletic than Just Wearing One Pair of Shoes," Costanoa Ventures, March 13, 2017, https://www.costanoavc.com /steve-young-life-is-more-athletic-than-just-wearing-one -pair-of-shoes/; also see medium.com, https://medium .com/costanoa-ventures/life-is-more-athletic-than-just -wearing-one-pair-of-shoes-7fafbbc4c98f.

2. CONDITIONING:
THE BODY

1. Bob Bowman video interview with the *Washington Post*, "The Psychology of Speed," June 14, 2012, https://www .youtube.com/watch?v=Htw780vHH0o.
2. Author interview with Bob Bowman, February 14, 2020.
3. Adam Hadazy, "What Makes Michael Phelps So Good," *Scientific American*, August 18, 2008.
4. Kevin Cashman, "Resilience Trends at the Top: Fat Cats No More," *Forbes*, May 10, 2019; Dominic Barton, Andrew Grant, and Michelle Horn, "Leading in the 21st Century," *McKinsey Quarterly*, June 1, 2012, 30–47.
5. Michael W. Richardson, "How Much Energy Does the Brain Use?," February 1, 2019, Society for Neuroscience, Brainfacts.org, https://www.brainfacts.org/brain-anatomy -and-function/anatomy/2019/how-much-energy-does-the -brain-use-020119.
6. Author interview with Bob Iger, June 2, 2021.
7. Anthony King, "Could Mitochondria Help Athletes Make Gains?," *Nature* 592 (April 1, 2021): 57–59; "How Exercise—Interval Training in Particular—Helps Your Mitochondria Stave Off Old Age," ScienceDaily, March 7,

2017, Cell Press, https://www.sciencedaily.com/releases /2017/03/170307155214.htm.

8. Richardson, "How Much Energy Does the Brain Use?"; Jessica M. Appler and Lisa V. Goodrich, "Connecting the Ear to the Brain: Molecular Mechanisms of Auditory Circuit Assembly," *Progressive Neurobiology*, no. 93(4) (April 2011): 488–508.

9. Yaakov Stern, Anna MacKay-Brandt, Seonjoo Lee, Paula McKinley, Kathleen McIntyre, Qolamreza Razlighi, Emil Agarunov, Matthew Bartels, Richard P. Sloan, "Effect of Aerobic Exercise on Cognition in Younger Adults: A Randomized Clinical Trial," *Neurology* 92(9) (February 29, 2019).

10. "Leg Exercise Is Critical to Brain and Nervous System Health," *Science Daily*; Raffaella Adami, Jessica Pagano, Michela Colombo, Natalia Platonova, Deborah Recchia, Raffaella Chiaramonte, Roberto Bottinelli, Monica Canepari, and Daniele Bottai, "Reduction of Movement in Neurological Diseases: Effects on Neural Stem Cells Characteristics," *Frontiers in Neuroscience*, 2018.

11. Daniel Longman, Jay T. Stock, and Jonathan C. K. Wells, "A Trade-Off between Cognitive and Physical Performance, with Relative Preservation of Brain Function," *Scientific Reports*, published online October 20, 2017.

12. Author interview with Bob Bowman, February 14, 2020

13. Author interview with Michael Phelps for the *Washington Post*, June 14, 2012.

14. John Kiely, "A New Understanding of Stress and Implications for Our Cultural Training Paradigm," *New Studies in Athletics*, no. 3 (2015): 27–35.

15. Aaron J. Cunanan, Brad H. DeWeese, John P. Wagle, Kevin M. Carroll, Robert Sausaman, W. Guy Hornsby, G. Gregory Haff, N. Travis Triplett, Kyle C. Pierce, Michael H. Stone, "The General Adaptation Syndrome: A Foundation for the Concept of Periodization," *Sports Medicine* 48(4) (April 2018):787; Kiely, "A New Understanding of Stress."

16. Author interview with Bob Bowman, February 14, 2020; Bob Bowman (with Michael J. Stott), "Learn from the Olympians: Swim Like Mike," *Swimming Technique*, January–March 2003, 8–13.

17. Author interview with Michael Phelps, June 14, 2012; Michael Phelps video interview with the *Washington Post*, "The Psychology of Speed," June 14, 2012.

18. A. Trecroci, G. Boccolini, M. Duca, D. Formenti, and G. Alberti, "Mental Fatigue Impairs Physical Activity, Technical and Decision-Making Performance during Small-Sided Games," *PLOS One* 15(9), September 9, 2020, https://journals.plos.org/plosone/article?id=10.1371/journal.pone.023846; Leonardo Sousa Fortes, Petrus Gantois, Dalton de Lima-Júnior, Bruno Teixeira Barbosa, Maria Elisa Caputo, Fabio Yuzo Nakamura, Maicon R. Albuquerque, Fabiano Souza Fonseca, "Playing Videogames or Using Social Media Applications on Smartphones Causes Mental Fatigue and Impairs Decision-Making Performance in Amateur Boxers," *Applied Neuropsychology: Adult*, June 1, 2021, 1–12.

19. Author interview with Michael Phelps for the *Washington Post*, June 14, 2012.

20. Ibid.

21. Author interview with Bob Bowman, Febraury 14, 2020

22. Author interview with Michael Phelps for the *Washington Post*, June 14, 2012.

23. Ibid.

24. Author interview with Bob Bowman, February 14, 2020.

25. Author interview with Michael Sofis, behavioral health researcher, Advocates for Human Potential Inc., October 21, 2021; Sally Jenkins, "Tom Brady's Secret Is Self-Discipline," *Washington Post*, November 12, 2021.

26. Jack Kroll, "Stanley Kubrick's Horror Show," *Newsweek*, June 2, 1980.

27. Aishwarya Kumar, "The Grandmaster Diet: How to Lose Weight While Barely Moving," September 13, 2019, ESPN .com.

28. Kumar, "The Grandmaster Diet."

29. Charlotte Leedy and Leroy Dubeck, "The Effects of Tournament Chess Playing on Selected Physiological Responses in Players of Varying Aspects and Abilities" (Temple University, 1975); Charlotte Leedy and Leroy Dubeck, "Physiological Changes during Tournament Chess," *Chess Life and Review*, 1971, 708; V. Glezerov and E. Sobol, "Hygienic Evaluation of the Changes in Work Capacity of Young Chess Players during Training," *Gigiena I Sanitariia*, no. 24 (1987).

30. Frank Brady, *Bobby Fischer: Profile of a Prodigy* (New York: David McKay, 1965), 212.

31. Leon Watson, "Is Chess a Sport?," *Chessable* (blog), October 24, 2018, chessable.com.

32. "Magnus Carlsen Crushes in Las Vegas Chess Simuli," chessdom.com, January 10, 2014.

33. John Henderson, "Pulsating Play," firstmovechess.org, February 13, 2018; Marissa Payne, "World Chess Wants to Hook Up Grandmasters to Heart Monitors to Make Matches 'More Exciting,'" *Washington Post*, August 10, 2017.

34. Kumar, "The Grandmaster Diet"; Josh St. Clair, "How Elite Chess Players Can Burn More Than 6,000 Calories Sitting Down," *Men's Health*, September 20, 2019; Jen Murphy, "How a Chess Champion Trains for the Big Game," *Wall Street Journal*, November 14, 2016; "Magnus Carlsen: Daily Routine," balancethegrind.com, November 19, 2020.

35. Brendan M. Lynch, "New Study Links Exercise to Better Self-Control," Kansas University News Service, September 5, 2017; M. J. Sofis, A. Carrillo, and D. P. Jarmolowicz, "Maintained Physical Activity Induced Changes in Delay Discounting," *Behavior Modification* 41(4) (2017): 499–528; author interview with Michael Sofis, October 21, 2021.

36. Author interview with Dana Cavalea, September 28, 2021; Dana Cavalea, *Habits of a Champion* (Stamford, CT: Dana Cavalea Companies, 2018), 27.
37. Eden B. King, Steven G. Rogelberg, Michelle R. Hebl, Phillip W. Braddy, Linda R. Shanock, Sharon C. Doerer, Sharon McDowell-Larsen, "Waistlines and Ratings of Executives: Does Executive Status Overcome Obesity Stigma?," *Human Resource Management* 55, no. 2 (March–April 2016): 283–300.
38. Author interview with Laird Hamilton, October 12, 2020
39. Firdaus S. Dhabhar, "The Short-Term Stress Response: Mother Nature's Mechanism for Enhancing Protection and Performance under Conditions of Threat, Challenge and Opportunity," *Frontiers in Neuroendocrinology* 49 (April 2018): 175–92; Firdaus S. Dhabhar, "The Power of Positive Stress—a Complementary Commentary," *Stress* 22(5) (September 2019): 526–29; Kristin Sainani, "What, Me Worry? Why You Should Stop Sweating Everyday Aggravations and Embrace the Benefits of Stress," *Stanford Magazine*, May–June 2014.
40. Kelly McGonigal, "Can We Reframe the Way We Think about Stress?," NPR, August 2, 2019, npr.com.

3. PRACTICE:
THE MIND

1. Ricky Jay, *Learned Pigs and Fireproof Women* (New York: Villard Books, 1986), 85.
2. Sally Jenkins, "Racket Science," *Sports Illustrated*, April 29, 1991, https://vault.si.com/vault/1991/04/29/racket-science-billie-jean-king-has-been-a-dynamo-as-a-tennis-champion-promoter-television-commentator-businesswoman-and-feminist-but-she-may-be-even-more-compelling-in-her-latest-career-teaching.

3. Author email exchange with Mark Cuban, September 28, 2021.

4. Author interview with Peyton Manning, April 18, 2022

5. John Wooden and Don Yaeger, *A Game Plan for Life: The Power of Mentoring* (New York: Bloomsbury, 2009), 150.

6. Tom Brady interview, Adobe Summit Q&A 2020.

7. Bill Walsh, Brian Billick, and James Peterson, *Finding the Winning Edge* (Champaign, IL: Sports Publishing), 207; Bill Walsh, "When Things Go Bad," *Forbes*, March 29, 1993.

8. Tom Brady interview, Adobe Summit Q&A 2020.

9. Peter King, "Driving the 101 with Sean McVay," Peter King's Football Morning in America, January 28, 2019, profootballtalk.nbc.com.

10. Author interview with Lawyer Milloy for the *Washington Post, August 5, 2018*; Jenkins, "Football Is Changing."

11. Author interview with Reggie Wayne for the *Washington Post, August 5, 2018*; Sally Jenkins, "The Patriots' Secret Is Focusing on the Details. Every. Last. Detail," *Washington Post*, January 31, 2019.

12. Author interview with Bill Belichick for the *Washington Post*, August 5, 2018.

13. *Bill Belichick's School of Coaching: Discipline & Trust*, NFL Films, December 1, 2017; Bill Belichick interview with Suzy Welch, CNBC, April 13, 2017.

14. "Pats Linebacker Adalius Thomas Discusses Being Sent Home," ESPNBoston.com, December 10, 2009.

15. *Bill Belichick's School of Coaching.*

16. Author interview with Lawyer Milloy, August 5, 2018; Jenkins, "The Patriots' Secret."

17. Jenkins, "The Patriots' Secret."

18. Bill Barnwell, "Fact-Checking Patriots' 18-year Dynasty: What's Real, What's Myth," ESPN.com, January 18, 2019; Zach Kram, "Patriots Conspiracy Theories," theringer.com, January 28, 1018.

19. "The Patriots Decade of Dominance by the Numbers," patriots.com, December 31, 2019.

20. Author interview with Peyton Manning, April 18, 2022

21. Super Bowl MVP press conference, Atlanta, February 4, 2019.

22. Author interview with Peyton Manning, April 18, 2022.

23. Author correspondence with Dr. Sian Beilock, December 13, 2011, subsequent email correspondence with Dr. Beilock, November 23, 2020.

24. K. Anders Ericsson and Kyle Harwell, "Deliberate Practice and Proposed Limits on the Effects of Practice on the Acquisition of Expert Performance: Why the Original Definition Matters and Recommendations for Future Research," *Frontiers of Psychology*, October 25, 2019.

25. Ibid.

26. Ulrik Juul Christensen, "Why Corporate Learning Needs Ericsson's Deliberate Practice More Than Ever," *Forbes*, June 22, 2020.

27. David Fleming, "No More Questions," oral history of Bill Belichick for ESPN.com, October 4, 2016.

28. Author interview with Tom House, April 16, 2021; Sally Jenkins, "Deflategate Got Tom Brady Mad, and Now the Rest of the NFL Is Paying the Price," *Washington Post*, November 6, 2015; "Tom Brady Pass Completion Percentage Career," statmuse.com, https://www.statmuse .com/nfl/ask/tom-brady-pass-completion-percentage-career.

29. Ibid.

30. Sian L. Beilock, Ian M. Lyons, Andrew Mattarella-Micke, Howard C. Nusbaum, and Steven L. Small, "Sports Experience Changes the Neural Processing of Action Language," *Proceedings of the National Academy of Sciences*, September 8, 2008.

31. Bruce Abernethy, "Training the Visual-Perceptual Skills of Athletes: Insights from the Study of Motor Expertise," *American Journal of Sports Medicine*, November 1, 1996; David Epstein, "It's All about Anticipation," *Sports Illustrated*, August 8, 2011.

32. Author interview with Dr. Sian Leah Beilock, December 13, 2011.

33. Author interview with Bob Behnken for the *Washington Post*, October 21, 2011; Sally Jenkins, "College Football Helped Mike Hopkins Prepare for the International Space Station," *Washington Post*, December 26, 2013.

34. Author interview with Bob Behnken, October 21, 2011.

35. Author interview with Dr. Sian Leah Beilock, December 13, 2011, email correspondence. November 24, 2020; Alexandra Wolfe, "An Expert Take on Performing under Pressure," *Wall Street Journal*, February 23, 2017, https:// www.wsj.com/articles/an-expert-take-on-performing -under-pressure-1486147854; Sian Leah Beilock, "How Not to Choke under Pressure," ideas.ted.com, April 8, 2019, https://ideas.ted.com/how-not-to-choke-under-pressure.

36. Author interview with Dr. Sian Leah Beilock, December 13, 2011.

37. Ibid.

38. Beilock, "How Not to Choke under Pressure."

39. Sian Beilock and Thomas H. Carr, "On the Fragility of Skilled Performance: What Governs Choking under Pressure," *Journal of Experimental Psychology: General* 130, no. 4 (2001): 701–25.

40. Beilock et al., "Sports Experience Changes the Neural Processing of Action Language.

41. Author interview with Dr. Sian Leah Beilock, December 13, 2011.

42. Author interview with Frank Reich, March 31 2020.

43. Author interview with Tom House, April 16, 2021.

44. Author interview with Leigh Steinberg, April 16, 2021.

45. Author interview with Tom House, April 16, 2021.

46. Henry Davis IV, Mario Liotti, Elton T. Ngan, Todd S. Woodward, Jared X. Van Snellenberg, Sari M. van Anders, Aynsley Smith, and Helen S. Mayberg, "fMRI

BOLD Signal Changes in Elite Swimmers While Viewing Videos of Personal Failure," *Brain Imaging and Behavior*, December 10, 2007; "Hap Davis Talk: Five Points of Better Racing," *LYNX Triathlon* (blog), January 16, 2020, https://lynxtriathlon.ca/2020/01/16/hap-davis-talk-five-points-of -better-racing/; Sian Beilock, "How the Anxiety and Stress of Messing Up Something Big Can Be Vanquished," NBC News, think.nbcnews.com, August 2, 2019.

47. Author interview with Dr. Sian Leah Beilock, December 13, 2011.

48. Christensen, "Why Corporate Learning Needs Ericsson's Deliberate Practice More than Ever."

49. Author interview with Pia Nilsson and Lynn Marriott, October 10, 2020.

50. "Pettersen Keeps Cool in a Major Way," *Tampa Bay Times*, June 11, 2007.

4. DISCIPLINE:
THE FRAMEWORK

1. Doc Rivers, *Flying Coach* podcast with Steve Kerr and Pete Carroll, theringer.com, June 16, 2020.

2. Doc Rivers, "What I've Learned in 20 Seasons as an NBA Head Coach," theundefeated.com, November 28, 2018.

3. Ibid.

4. Steve Kerr and Doc Rivers exchange, *Flying Coach* podcast with Steve Kerr and Pete Carroll, theringer.com, June 16, 2020.

5. Ibid.

6. Author interview with Bob Iger, June 2, 2021.

7. Kalyn Kahler, "When the Patriot Way Goes Wrong," Bleacher Report, November 13, 2020, https://bleacherreport.com /articles/2917777-how-matt-patricias-patriot-way-went-the -wrong-way-in-detroit.

8. Ibid.
9. Ibid.
10. Robert Hogan and Robert B. Kaiser, "What We Know about Leadership," *Review of General Psychology* 9, no. 2 (2005); 173, copyright by the Educational Publishing Foundation.
11. Ibid.
12. Author interview with Steve Kerr, April 16, 2020.
13. Ibid.; Steve Jamison, *Wooden on Leadership* (New York: McGraw Hill Education, 2005),114.
14. Jamison, *Wooden on Leadership*, 114.
15. Author interview with Steve Kerr, April 16, 2020.
16. Ibid.
17. Ibid.; Kerr interview with Positive Coaching Alliance, "Advice to Sports Parents from Steve Kerr," poscoach.org.
18. Mike Krzyzewski on his website, CoachK.com; Greg Dale interview with Mike Krzyzewski, "Coach K on Credible Coaching," Championship Coaches Network, championshipcoachesnetwork.com.
19. Mike Krzyzewski, CoachK.com.
20. Greg Dale interview with Mike Krzyzewski, "Coach K on Credible Coaching."
21. Mike Krzyzewski postgame press conference, December 21, 2016.
22. Radio interview with Mike Krzyzewski, *The Dan Patrick Show*, December 22, 2016; Mike Krzyzewski interview with Seth Davis, SI.com, Dec. 22, 2016.
23. Grayson Allen to JJ Reddick, *The Old Man and the Three* (podcast), September 28, 2020; Mike Krzyzewski to JJ Reddick, *The Old Man and the Three*, October 14, 2020.
24. Steve Wiseman, "Grayson Allen Said He Had a Roller-Coaster Duke Career. Coach K Had Another Word for It," *News & Observer*, April 20, 2018.
25. Dan Patrick interview with Mike Krzyzewski, December 22, 2020; Tim Keown, "Coach K Leads Duke Back to the

Final Four for One More College Ritual," March 27, 2022, ESPN.com, https://www.espn.com/mens-college -basketball/story/_/id/33589314/coach-k-leads-duke-back -final-four-one-more-college-basketball-ritual.

26. Grayson Allen at NBA Draft combine press conference, May 18, 2018; Steve Wiseman, "Grayson Allen Said He Had a Roller-Coaster Duke Career. Coach K Had Another Word for It," *News & Observer*, April 20, 2018.
27. Mike Krzyzewski to JJ Reddick, *The Old Man and the Three* (podcast), October 14, 2020.
28. Author interview with Pat Summitt for Pat Summitt with Sally Jenkins, *Reach for the Summit: The Definite Dozen System for Succeeding at Whatever You Do* (New York: Three Rivers Press, 1998), 92.
29. Author conversations with Pat Summitt.
30. Summitt, *Reach for the Summit*, 100; author conversations with Pat Summitt.
31. Author conversations with Pat Summitt.
32. Sally Jenkins, "Why Do We Let Immigrants from 'Holes' into Our Country? Because of People like This," *Washington Post*, January 12, 2018; Maria Cornelius, "Nicky Anosike: 'This Is Home,'" GoVols247, August 23, 2018.
33. Cornelius, "Nicky Anosike."
34. Dan Fleser, "UT's Nicky Anosike Will Serve as Model Lady Vol in Role as Graduate Assistant," knoxnews.com, August 24, 2018.
35. Author conversations with Pat Summitt.
36. Cornelius, "Nicky Anosike."
37. Author interview with Muffet McGraw, May 20, 2020.
38. Ibid.
39. Pete Carroll, *Flying Coach* podcast, theringer.com, April 13, 2020.
40. Kathleen Gray and Shawn Hubler, "Notre Dame's President Faces an Angry Campus after Getting the Coronavirus," *New York Times*, October 7, 2020.

41. Lilah Burke, "Are Colleges Superspreaders?," insidehighered.com, January 13, 2021.

42. Patricia McGuire, "The Moral Failure of Father Jenkins," *Chronicle of Higher Education*, October 8, 2020, https://www.chronicle.com/article/the-moral-failure-of-father-john-jenkins.

43. Author interview with Bob Iger, June 2, 2021.

44. Hogan and Kaiser, "What We Know about Leadership," 173.

45. Author interview with Dana Cavalea, September 28, 2021.

46. Ibid.

47. Ibid.

48. Ibid.

49. Ibid.

50. Cavalea, *Habits of a Champion*, 24.

51. H. A. Dorfman, *The Mental ABCs of Pitching* (Lanham, MD: Globe Pequot, 2016), 90.

5. CANDOR:

THE LANGUAGE

1. George Bainton, ed., *The Art of Authorship: Literary Reminiscences, Methods of Work, and Advice to Young Beginners* (New York, Appleton, 1890), 87.

2. Author interviews with and correspondence with Bonnie Stoll, October 14, 2020, and email interview-exchange with Diana Nyad, July 12, 2021.

3. Mintzberg, Raisinghani, and Theoret, "The Structure of 'Unstructured' Decision Processes."

4. Author interview with Bonnie Stoll, October 14, 2020.

5. Author interview and correspondence with Diana Nyad, July 12, 2021.

6. Ariel Levy, "Breaking the Waves," *The New Yorker*, February 2, 2014.

7. Author email interview with Diana Nyad, July 12, 2021.

8. Sally Jenkins, "Diana Nyad, at Age 61, Prepares for Second Attempt to Swim from Cuba to Key West," *Washington Post*, May 26, 2011.
9. Nyad interview in documentary film *The Other Shore*, directed by Timothy Wheeler, 2013.
10. Author email correspondence with Diana Nyad, July 12, 2021.
11. Ibid.
12. Exchange appeared in *The Other Shore*.
13. Ibid.
14. Incident appeared in *The Other Shore*.
15. Ibid.; Author interview with Bonnie Stoll, October 14, 2020; Levy, "Breaking the Waves."
16. Author interview with Bonnie Stoll, October 14, 2020.
17. Ibid.
18. Ibid.
19. Author email correspondence with Diana Nyad, July 12, 2021.
20. Author interview with Bonnie Stoll, October 14, 2020.
21. Author correspondence with Diana Nyad, July 12, 2021.
22. Author interview with Bonnie Stoll, October 14, 2020.
23. Author email correspondence with Diana Nyad, July 12, 2021.
24. Ibid.; Lizette Alvarez, "Sharks Absent, Swimmer, 64, Strokes from Cuba to Florida," *New York Times*, September 2, 2013.
25. Robert B. Kaiser, Robert Hogan, and S. Bartholomew Craig, "Leadership and the Fate of Organizations," *American Psychologist* 63, no.2 (February–March 2008): 96–110.
26. From Sands, "Life Is More Athletic."
27. Ron Leuty, "49ers Legend Steve Young's Playbook for Entrepreneurial Success," *San Francisco Business Times*, May 26, 2020, https://www.bizjournals.com/sanfrancisco/news/2020/05/26/steve-young-san-francisco-49ers-hggc-bill-walsh.html.
28. From Sands, "Life Is More Athletic."
29. Ibid.

30. Ibid.
31. Author interview with Tony Dungy, September 15, 2020.
32. Paul C. Nutt, "Breaking out of the Failure Mode with Best Practice Decision-Making Processes," *International Journal of Business* 8, no. 2 (2003): 170–90.
33. Greg Dale interview with Mike Krzyzewski, "Coach K on Credible Coaching."
34. Nutt, "Breaking out of the Failure Mode," 170–90.
35. Chris Ballard, "The Little Book That Shaped the Minds of Steve Kerr and Pete Carroll," *Sports Illustrated*, May 26, 2016.
36. Tim Bontemps, "Steve Kerr Didn't Disrespect the Suns by Letting His Players Coach. He Was Waking Up the Warriors," *Washington Post*, February 13, 2018.
37. Author interview with Steve Kerr, April 16, 2020.
38. Ibid.
39. Author interview with Tony Dungy, September 15, 2020.
40. Ibid.
41. Steve Kerr, *Flying Coach*: podcast, theringer.com, April 17, 2020.
42. Howard Beck, "Kerr and Draymond Green's Relationship Nearly Destroyed the Warriors; Now It Fuels Them," bleacherreport.com, May 24, 2018, https://bleacherreport.com/articles/2777471-kerr-and-draymonds-relationship-nearly-destroyed-warriors-now-it-fuels-them.
43. Author interview with Steve Kerr, April 16, 2020.
44. Beck, "Kerr and Draymond Green's Relationship."
45. Matt Eppers, "Draymond Green Dismisses Warriors Turmoil: We're Still Going to Win the Championship," *USA Today*, November 16, 2018.
46. "Dak Prescott," *In Depth with Graham Bensinger*, September 9, 2020, https://grahambensingercom/2021/08/02/dak-prescott/.
47. Sally Jenkins, "Dak Prescott Delivered a Hell of a Message This Season, and It Will Outlast His Injury," *Washington Post*, October 12, 2020.

48. Jori Epstein, "Dak Prescott on Why He Opened Up about Depression, Brother's Suicide: Being a Leader Is about Being Genuine," *USA Today*, September 11, 2020.
49. Brené Brown to Pete Carroll and Steve Kerr, *Flying Coach* podcast, theringer.com, April 20, 2020.

6. CULTURE:
THE ENVIRONMENT

1. Steve Kerr, *Flying Coach* podcast, theringer.com, episode 1, April 13, 2020.
2. Author interview with Steve Kerr, April 16, 2020.
3. Steve Kerr and Pete Carroll, *Flying Coach* podcast, theringer.com, June 3, 2020.
4. Bill Walsh, Steve Jamison, and Craig Walsh, *The Score Takes Care of Itself* (New York: Portfolio, 2009), 15.
5. Sands, "Life Is More Athletic."
6. David Wharton, "Pete Carroll's Basic Instinct," *Los Angeles Times*, August 1, 2001.
7. Pete Carroll, *Flying Coach* podcast, theringer.com, April 3, 2020.
8. Steve Kerr, *Flying Coach* podcast, theringer.com, April 3, 2020.
9. Phil Jackson, Twitter, February 9, 2016.
10. Author interview with Steve Kerr, April 16, 2020; Phil Jackson and Hugh Delehanty, *Eleven Rings: The Soul of Success* (New York: Penguin Press, 2013) 80–85.
11. Steve Kerr, *Flying Coach* podcast, theringer.com, April 28, 2020.
12. Author interview with Steve Kerr, April 16, 2020; Steve Kerr, *Flying Coach* podcast, theringer.com, April 28, 2020.
13. Jackson and Delehanty, *Eleven Rings*, 84.
14. Author interview with Steve Kerr, April 16, 2020.
15. Author personal conversation with Pat Summitt.

16. Author interview with Mary Karr December 22, 2014; Sally Jenkins, "Phil Jackson, Pat Summitt, Mary Karr and a Special Triangular Connection," *Washington Post*, January 1, 2016.

17. Ross Robertson, "The Soul of Teamwork: An Interview with Phil Jackson," *What Is Enlightenment?*, issue 25 (2004).

18. Steve Kerr, *Flying Coach* podcast, theringer.com, June 3, 2020.

19. Steve Kerr, *Flying Coach* podcast, theringer.com, episode 1; author interview with Steve Kerr; Melissa Rohlin, "Steve Kerr and Gregg Popovich Open Up about Their Relationship," bayareanewsgroup.com, March 7, 2018.

20. Gregg Popovich pregame press conference, San Antonio versus Boston, October 31, 2017; Paul Flannery, "Gregg Popovich Holds Court," sbnation.com, October 31, 2017.

21. NBA TV interview with Gregg Popovich, "Champions Revealed: 2014 San Antonio Spurs," October 27, 2014; Marc J. Spears, "Gregg Popovich Is the NBA's Most Woke Coach," *The Undefeated* podcast, November 9, 2016.

22. Author interview with Steve Kerr, April 16, 2020.

23. Gregg Popovich *Flying Coach* podcast, theringer.com, June 3, 2020.

24. Michael Lee Stallard, "NBA Spurs Culture Creates Competitive Advantage," Fox Business, February 25, 2015; Gregg Popovich, *Flying Coach* podcast, theringer.com, June 3, 2020; Baxter Holmes, "Michelin Restaurant and Fabulous Wines: Inside the Secret Team Dinners That Have Built the Spurs Dynasty," ESPN.com, July 25, 2020.

25. Gregg Popovich, *Flying Coach* podcast, theringer.com, June 3, 2020.

26. Steve Kerr, *Flying Coach* podcast, theringer.com," June 3, 2020.

27. Ibid.

28. Author interview with Steve Kerr, April 16, 2020.

29. Steve Kerr interview, Dean's Executive Leadership Series, Pepperdine University, March 21, 2017.

30. Author interview with Steve Kerr, April 16, 2020; Steve Kerr interview, Dean's Executive Leadership Series, Pepperdine University, March 21, 2017; Chris Ballard, "Warriors: From One Dimensional and One and Done to NBA Title Favorites," *Sports Illustrated*, February 18, 2015.

31. Author interview with Steve Kerr, April 16, 2020; Steve Kerr interview, Dean's Executive Leadership Series, Pepperdine University, March 21, 2017.

32. Steve Kerr, *Flying Coach* podcast, theringer.com, April 13, 2020.

33. Ibid.

34. Connor Letourneau, "What Sets Warriors Practice Apart in the NBA? Mix Some E-40 with Aretha Franklin," *San Francisco Chronicle*, February 5, 2019.

35. Ramona Shelburne, ESPN, "LOL with the Warriors Staff," ESPN.com, June 3, 2015; Ballard, "Warriors"; Scott Cacciola, "For the Golden State Warriors, Practice Makes Perfect Silliness," *New York Times*, May 30, 2015.

36. Ben Cohen, "Golden State: The Team That Eats Together," *Wall Street Journal*, February 11, 2015; Jordan Brenner, "The Warriors Secret Sauce? Team Diners on the Road," ESPN.com, April 10, 2016.

37. Ballard, "Warriors."

38. Author interview with Steve Kerr, April 16, 2020.

39. Shelburne, "LOL with the Warriors Staff."

40. Author interview with Steve Kerr, April 16, 2020.

41. Ibid.

42. Steve Kerr interview, Dean's Executive Leadership Series, Pepperdine University, March 21, 2017.

43. Boris Groysberg, Jeremiah Lee, Jesse Price, and J. Yo-Jud Cheng, "The Leader's Guide to Corporate Culture," *Harvard Business Review*, January–February 2018, 44–52.

44. Courtney Majocha, "Steve Kerr Holds Court at Harvard Law," *Harvard Law Today*, April 13, 2022, today.law

.harvard.com https://today.law.harvard.edu/steve-kerr
-holds-court-at-harvard-law/.

45. Groysberg et al., "The Leader's Guide to Corporate
    Culture."

46. Author interview with Ron Rivera, April 13, 2021.

47. Scott Mautz, "Patagonia Has Only 4 Percent Employee
    Turnover Because They Value This One Thing So Much,"
    Inc.com, https://www.inc.com/scott-mautz/how-can
    -patagonia-have-only-4-percent-worker-turnover-hint
    -they-pay-activist-employees-bail.html; https://www
    .greatplacetowork.com/certified-company/1000745.

48. Barbara S. Christen and Steven Flanders, eds., *Cass
    Gilbert, Life and Work: Architect of the Public Domain*
    (New York, London: W. W. Norton, 2001), 65.

49. John Powers, "A Brief History of Athletics at Harvard,"
    October 11, 2016, Harvard University athletic department
    website, https://gocrimson.com/sports/2020/5/5/General
    -Core-Values-athletics-history.aspx?id=10.

50. Ibid.

51. John Powers, "A Good, Long Run," *Harvard Gazette*, May
    29, 2020.

52. Caleb W. Peiffer, "Players, Committee Meets with
    Amaker," *Harvard Crimson*, April 6, 2007; Ted Kirby, "The
    Amaker Era Begins," *Harvard Crimson*, April 15, 2007.

53. John Feinstein, "Duke's Amaker Shows the Mark of a
    Winner," *Washington Post*, January 14, 1987.

54. Author interview with Tommy Amaker, August 26, 2020.

55. Ibid.

56. Nathan Fenno, "Who Is Tommy Amaker?," *Ann Arbor
    News*, March 17, 2007.

57. Tommy Amaker, "2020 Vision," *Harvard Crimson*, June
    10, 2020.

58. Author interview with Tommy Amaker, August 26, 2020;
    "Harvard's Amaker Honored with Two Major Awards for
    Diversity and Inclusion," ivyleague.com, March 24, 2021.

59. Jeff Bezos, Letter to Amazon shareholders, 2017.
60. Anna Katherine Clemmons, "Brandyn Curry Makes a Name at Harvard," *Charlotte Magazine*, February 22, 2012.
61. Tommy Amaker, "Practice Planning and Teaching Methodology," NABC *Time-Out* magazine, January 12, 2021.
62. Author interview with Tommy Amaker, August 26, 2020.
63. Ibid.
64. Ibid.
65. Ibid.; Christina Pazzanese, "The New Breakfast Club," *Harvard Gazette*, March 4, 2021.
66. Author interview with Tommy Amaker, August 26, 2020; Pazzanese, "The New Breakfast Club"; Jimmy Golen, "For Harvard Coach Tommy Amaker, Class Is Always in Session," Associated Press, November 10, 2020.
67. Pablo S. Torre, "Harvard School of Basketball," *Sports Illustrated*, February 1, 2010; Jonathan Soroff, "The Interview: with Harvard Basketball Coach Tommy Amaker," *Boston* magazine, November 9, 2020.
68. Peter May, "Harvard Basketball Seeks First Ivy League Basketball Title," *New York Times*, March 3, 2011.
69. Bob Ryan, "Crimson Do Their Part When Needed," *Boston Globe*, March 6, 2011.
70. Author interview with Tommy Amaker, August 26, 2020.
71. Ibid.; Amaker, "2020 Vision."
72. Author interview with Tommy Amaker, August 26, 2020.
73. Ibid.
74. Ibid.

7. FAILURE:
THE TEACHER

1. Sally Jenkins, "The Lasting Lesson of This Super Bowl: Failure Is Necessary," *Washington Post*, February 4, 2020.

2. Ibid.; Sally Jenkins, "From LeBron James to Phil Mickelson: First Place Rewards but Second Place Teaches," *Washington Post*, June 21, 2013.
3. Dan Graziano, "NFL Training Camps: Fantasy Football Tips, Nuggets, and What I Learned at the Bills, Steelers, Lions and Browns Stops," ESPN, August 7, 2021, https://www.espn.com/nfl/insider/insider/story/_/id/31974572/nfl-training-camps-fantasy-football-tips-nuggets-learned-bills-steelers-browns-lions-stops.
4. Jenkins, "The Lasting Lesson of This Super Bowl"; Jenkins, "From LeBron James to Phil Mickelson."
5. Paul C. Nutt, "Learning from Failed Decisions," *Performance Improvement Quarterly* 23 (3): 15–38.
6. Ibid., 16.
7. Ibid., 32–33.
8. Ibid.
9. Paul C. Nutt, *Why Decisions Fail: Avoiding the Blunders and Traps That Lead to Debacles* (San Francisco: Berrett Koehler, 2002), 313–15.
10. Author interview with Steve Kerr, April 16, 2020.
11. Ibid.
12. Ibid.
13. Majocha, "Steve Kerr Holds Court at Harvard."
14. David Kenyon, "Ranking the Most Clutch NBA Players since 2000," Bleacher Report, November 26, 2021, https://bleacherreport.com/articles/2950160-ranking-the-most-clutch-nba-players-since-2000.
15. Ibid.
16. Steve Kerr, *Flying Coach* podcast, theringer.com, April 28, 2020.
17. John Wooden and Steve Jamison, *Wooden: A Lifetime of Observations and Reflections on and off the Court* (New York: McGraw Hill, 1997), 80.
18. Author interview with Steve Kerr, April 16, 2020.

19. Ibid.
20. Kevin Kelly, "The Virtues of Negative Results," edge.com, https://www.edge.org/response-detail/10422.
21. Jeff Bezos, Letter to Amazon shareholders, 2013.
22. Jeff Bezos, Letter to Amazon shareholders, 2018.
23. Jeff Bezos at Business Insider Ignition Conference 2014; Samuel Gibbs, "Jeff Bezos: I've Made Billions of Dollars of Failures at Amazon," *Guardian*, December 3, 2014, https://www.theguardian.com/technology/2014/dec/03/jeff-bezos-billions-dollars-failures-amazon; Jeff Bezos, Letter to Amazon shareholders, 2015.
24. Yian Yin, Yang Wang, James A. Evans, and Dashun Wang, "Quantifying the Dynamics of Failure across Science, Startups and Security," *Nature* 575 (October 20, 2019): 190–94, https://www.nature.com/articles/s41586-019-1725-y.
25. Jeff Bezos, June 7, 2011, Amazon shareholder meeting.
26. Jeff Bezos, Letter to Amazon shareholders, 2008.
27. Author interview with David Cutcliffe, April 15, 2020.
28. Carli Lloyd at 2019 World Cup; Kevin Baxter, "Women's World Cup: U.S. Defeats Sweden in Its Group Play Finale," *Baltimore Sun*, June 20, 2019.
29. Author interview with Jill Ellis, March 25, 2020.
30. Ibid.
31. Ibid.
32. Author interview with Jill Ellis, March 25, 2020.
33. Nutt, "Breaking out of the Failure Mode," 186.
34. Seth Vertelney, "Captain of the Ship or Along for the Ride? How Much Credit Does Jill Ellis Get for the USWNT's Dominance?," goal.com, July 12, 2019, https://www.goal.com/en-us/news/captain-of-the-ship-or-along-for-the-ride-how-much-credit/luopliza54tj1nz8vfmkfmzdi.
35. Grant Wahl, "Ellis Deserves Praise but the Real Women's World Cup Starts Now," *Sports Illustrated*, June 19, 2019.
36. Author interview with Jill Ellis, March 5, 2020.
37. Author interview with Ron Rivera, April 13, 2021.

38. Author interview with Ron Rivera, April 13, 2021.
39. Alex Kennedy, "20-Year Study: Coaches in NBA Have Highest Turnover among Major Leagues," hoophype.com, May 5, 2019.
40. Jelena Kecmanovic, "How to Deal with Regret and Forgive Yourself for Making Imperfect Decisions," *Washington Post*, July 7, 2021.

8. INTENTION:
THE MOTIVE

1. Trevor Immelman, Twitter, February 8, 2021.
2. Sally Jenkins, "Tom Brady Still Has the Itch, and It's Taken Him to Places No Football Player Has Been," *Washington Post*, February 8, 2021.
3. Tom Brady interview, May 10, 2021, HODINKEE Radio, hodinkee.com; Sally Jenkins, "Deflategate Got Tom Brady Mad, and Now the Rest of the NFL Is Paying the Price," *Washington Post*, November 6, 2015; Sally Jenkins, "For Brady, Ordinary Values," *Washington Post*, January 16, 2005.
4. Richard Branson, *Richard Branson's Blog*, November 2016, https://www.virgin.com/branson-family/richard-branson-blog; Rose Leadem, "Richard Branson: The Key to Success Is Intention," entrepreneur.com, November 2, 2016, https://www.entrepreneur.com/article/284627.
5. Author interview with Tom Brady for the *Washington Post*, January 2, 2005; Jenkins, "For Brady, Ordinary Values."
6. Jenkins, "Deflategate Got Brady Mad"; Tom Brady Super Bowl press conference, February 3, 2021.
7. Jenkins, "Deflategate Got Brady Mad"; Tom Brady interview with James Brown, CBS, December 7, 2011, https://www.youtube.com/watch?v=qo3_AkD5BoQ; Tom Martinez passed away in 2012.
8. Jenkins, "For Brady, Ordinary Values."

9. Jenkins, "Deflategate Got Brady Mad."

10. Tom Brady, Adobe Summit Q&A 2020.

11. Jenkins, "For Brady, Ordinary Values."

12. Ibid.; Jenkins, "Tom Brady Is Telling His Own Story and Doing It at His Own Pace," *Washington Post*, January 15, 2022.

13. Rick Stroud, "How TB12 Keeps Tom Brady Ageless and Thriving in the NFL," *Tampa Bay Times*, September 28, 2021.

14. Author interview with Gotham Chopra, December 13, 2021; Jenkins, "Deflategate Got Brady Mad."

15. Sally Jenkins, "Tom Brady, with Discipline and Meticulous Planning, Put Aside the Indignity of Athletic Aging," *Washington Post*, November 2, 2020.

16. Qualtrics "WorkDifferent" 2021 seminar interview with Tom Brady, "Taking Small Actions to Deliver Big Wins," qualtrics.com, April 13, 2021, https://www.qualtrics.com/work-different/keynote-tom-brady/.

17. Bruce Arians Super Bowl press conference, February 5, 2021.

18. Donté Stallworth, Twitter, October 6, 2015.

19. Jenkins, "Tom Brady Still Has the Itch"; Todd Bowles Super Bowl press conference, February 5, 2021.

20. Michael Irvin, ESPN Super Bowl press conference, February 5, 2021.

21. Lavonte David interview on *All Things Considered* podcast, CBS, https://podcasts.apple.com/us/podcast/all-things-covered-lavonte-david-shares-emotions-when/id1263289980?i=1000507640356.

22. LeSean McCoy interview, *The Pat McAfee Show*, February 17, 2021, https://www.youtube.com/watch?v=Syt-TLC36fE.

23. Qualtrics, "Taking Small Actions."

24. Tom Brady, Super Bowl postgame interview, February 7, 2021.

25. Tom Brady Super Bowl Press conference, February 5, 2021.

26. Henry McKenna, "Tom Brady Explains Football Left Gisele Unsatisfied with Their Marriage," *USA Today*, April 8, 2020.

27. Tom Brady Super Bowl press conference, February 3, 2021.

28. Mike Florio, "Dolphins Planned to Pursue Sean Payton, Tom Brady for 2022," ProFootballTalk, NBCSports.com, https://profootballtalk.nbcsports.com/2022/02/28/dolphins-planned-to-pursue-sean-payton-tom-brady-for-2022/.

29. Sally Jenkins, "On Paper, Tom Brady Was Unremarkable. On the Field, He Grew into a Legend," *Washington Post*, February 1, 2022.

30. Qualtrics, "Taking Small Actions."

31. Author interview with Robert Hogan for the *Washington Post*, November 29, 2011; Sally Jenkins, "Tim Tebow Shows What Leadership Is," *Washington Post*, December 1, 2011.

32. Author interview with Robert Hogan, November 29, 2011; Hogan and Kaiser, "What We Know about Leadership," 173.

33. Susan T. Fiske and Cydney Dupree, "Gaining Trust as Well as Respect in Communicating to Motivated Audiences about Science Topics," *Proceedings of the National Academy of Sciences*, September 16, 2014.

34. Jack Zenger and Joseph Folkman, "I'm the Boss. Why Should I Care If You Like Me?," November 21, 2021, zengerfolkman.com.

35. Kaiser, Hogan, and Craig, "Leadership and the Fate of Organizations," 96–110.

36. Hallie Grossman and Michael DiRocco, "Inside Urban Meyer's Disastrous Tenure as Jacksonville Jaguars Coach," ESPN.com, December 17, 2021; Sally Jenkins, "Why Urban Meyer Is Failing with the Jacksonville Jaguars," *Washington Post*, December 14, 2021.

37. Amy J. C. Cuddy, Matthew Kohut, and John Neffinger, "Connect, Then Lead," *Harvard Business Review*, July–August 2013.

38. Christopher Boehm, "Political Primates," *Greater Good Magazine*, December 1, 2007, greatergood.berkeley.edu; Megan Gambino, "How Humans Became Moral Beings,"

interview with Christopher Boehm for *Smithsonian* magazine, May 3, 2012, smithsonianmag.com.

39. Pat Riley, *The Winner Within* (New York: G. P. Putnam's Sons, 1993), 60.

40. Sally Jenkins, "John Harbaugh Gets What Urban Meyer Missed," *Washington Post*, December 23, 2021.

41. Hogan, Kaiser, and Craig, "Leadership and the Fate of Organizations," 96–110.

42. Chantel Jennings, "Alone at the Summit: Kelly Harper Leads Lady Vols Back Where They Belong," *The Athletic*, February 3, 2022, https://theathletic.com/3101282 /2022/02/04/alone-at-the-summit-without-her-two -guiding-forces-kellie-harper-leads-lady-vols-back-where -they-belong/.

43. Meg James, "How Disney's Bob Iger Went from Underrated CEO to Hollywood Royalty," *Los Angeles Times*, March 1, 2020.

44. Brad Christian, "SOF Leader's Advice for Reaching Full Potential," February 8, 2019, thecipherbrief.com.

45. Tony Dungy official biography, Pro Football Hall of Fame, profootballhof.com.

46. Author interview with Tony Dungy, September 15, 2020.

47. Ibid.

48. Author interview with Peyton Manning, April 18, 2022.

49. Donnell Alexander, "Tony Dungy: Can This Nice Guy Finish First," Indianapolis Monthly, September 18, 2002.

50. Ibid.; Jeff Sullivan, "Tony Dungy's Children's Books Seek to Impact a New Generation," *Success* magazine, December 2, 2018.

51. Author interview with Tony Dungy, September 15, 2020.

52. Ibid.

53. Ibid.

54. Ibid.

55. Ibid.

56. Author interview with Peyton Manning, April 18, 2022.

57. Author interview with Peyton Manning, April 18, 2022.

58. Author interview with Tony Dungy, September 15, 2020; Andrew Walker, "Tony Dungy Recalls His Biggest 'Argument' With Peyton Manning," March 12, 2018, Colts.com.

59. Author interview with Tony Dungy, September 15, 2020.

60. Ibid.

61. Ibid.

62. Author interview with Peyton Manning, April 18, 2022.

63. Ibid.

64. Sally Jenkins, "If This Is Peyton Manning's Last Start, You Can Believe He'll Be Ready," *Washington Post*, February 16, 2016.

65. Reggie Wayne, interview with the NFL Network, June 29, 2017; Tony Dungy interview with radio host Anthony Calhoun, KRQE, *Big Game Bound* show, February 1, 2019, https://www.krqe.com/sports/the-big-game/tony-dungy-shares-peyton-manning-story-about-family-day/.

66. Ibid.

67. Ibid.

68. Ibid.

EPILOGUE:
THE HEART OF GREATNESS

1. Author interview with Steve Kerr, April 16, 2020.

2. Drew Shiller, "Kerr Enjoyed Warriors' 15-50 Season More Than Last NBA Finals Run," NBCSports.com, March 22, 2021.

3. Author interview with Laird Hamilton, October 12, 2020.

Index

INDEX

About the Author

SALLY JENKINS has been a *Washington Post* columnist and feature writer for nearly thirty years. She was a finalist for the Pulitzer Prize in 2019 and the winner of the Associated Press Red Smith Award for Outstanding Contributions to Sports Journalism in 2021. She has been named a columnist of the year five times by the Associated Press, and is the author of twelve books of non-fiction including *The Real All Americans*, *The State of Jones*, and the *New York Times* best seller *Sum It Up*, co-written with the late Pat Summitt. Jenkins also spent seven years as a senior writer for *Sports Illustrated* magazine, and other work has appeared in *Smithsonian*, GQ, *Tennis* magazine, *Golf Digest*, and *ESPN* magazine. In 2005, she was the first woman to be inducted into the National Sportscasters and Sportswriters Hall of Fame. She was presented for induction by her father, the late Dan Jenkins, also a Hall of Famer. She received her Bachelor of Arts degree from Stanford University in 1982 and resides in New York.